Short Memoirs of a Long Life

Esther Bogen

PAGE PUBLISHING, INC.
New York, NY

First originally published by Page Publishing, Inc. 2014

ISBN 978-1-62838-096-5 (pbk)
ISBN 978-1-62838-097-2 (digital)

Printed in the United States of America

Contents

A few months from now I will enter my 90th year. My body has aged appropriately; my movements are slower, my energy level is lower, and I sometimes walk into a room and have to rethink why I did so. Gratefully, my long term memory is still very acute. In that context, I can honestly say that all of the stories that appear here are true, factual, and personal. For the sake of discretion, the names of some of the characters have been changed to spare any embarrassment or discomfort to anyone connected to those persons.

Last night, in the midst of a nasty coughing spell brought on by a severe head cold, an old hidden memory suddenly resurfaced. I was nineteen years old, very much in love, and going to meet my future in-laws. I somewhat knew the mother; she was a customer in Bubby's store, a very heavy, peasant looking woman whose claim to fame was her ten children. But I had never met her on a personal basis.

The father was an enigma to me. What I did know about the father was that he was a little man with a Napoleon complex who had rules for the women in his family which were ludicrous. He did not approve of women wearing nail polish, so when his daughters were in his presence, they respected his rules. He did not abide lipstick, so again his rules were followed. Six of these seven sisters were married women and they allowed this despotic father to control them with these absurd attitudes. I had not met him yet, but I knew the tide had to shift, and I had to make it happen.

When I got to the house, with my polished nails and painted lips, I was confronted by a small man, half the size of his obese wife, sitting in an oversized chair waiting to see the prize his youngest son was bringing home. Of course in my favor, I was Mrs. Weinstein's grandchild. Mrs. Weinstein owned the most prestigious grocery store in the area so, had I been a dog, I would have had good papers. It served well for this little man that his son was going to marry a possible future heiress. Little men tend to revel in large prospects. The joke was on him because there was certainly no money to be inherited.

Although I was only nineteen and this man was in his sixties, I had instincts even then about men and how they liked to be treated. That I was tall, long legged, slim, and really good looking did not hamper me. When I got there, I was introduced, shyly acknowledged the introduction, and then carefully went about flirting with this old goat. Nothing inappropriate, of course, just some delicate whispered comments and sly smiles, like confidential intimacies. He fell right into the trap and was so excited that he started smoking one acrid foreign cigarette after another. The wretched thing hung from his lip, causing him to cough, choke, sputter, curse, and turn red and then purple. I thought he was going to die right there in front of me but nobody, neither wife nor children, paid any attention. I learned that he had been coughing like that for years. They took it in stride, but it really did not sit well with me.

A year later he died of emphysema. I never forgot that night, but it was well buried under so many other layers of life.

However, the other night when I was coughing, choking, sputtering, and swearing, that experience of many years ago resurfaced. I remember that reddish purple bulging face, and I ran into the bathroom to look at myself. By then, the spasm was over and all that was left was this ancient memory.

I have always been a good storyteller. A movie, a book,

a play, an incident, a joke, or a memory could be given life verbally, but I surely could not be a writer. That kind of commitment takes a certain ego and an accompanying discipline, which are both alien to me. One day, at a current events group, I met Rhoda Ferber who told me about a writer's workshop that she led at the Senior Center. Ridiculous as it may sound, going to the Senior Center was not very appealing, but I decided to give it a whirl. People are constantly encouraging me to write about my "checkered" life, so I got involved in the workshop and to my amazement, I discovered what great catharsis writing can be.

In evidence to that statement, I recalled that during a certain period in my life, when my son was still married to my granddaughter's mother, I wrote my daughter-in-law a long letter, telling her how I felt about her misbehavior as both a wife and especially as a mother. It was pretty spicy. After completing my diatribe, I put the document on my night table and gave a great sigh of relief. There it was, on paper, and I didn't have to agonize about it anymore, worrying that something must have been overlooked. Of course I never mailed the letter, but writing it was a great curative experience.

And so the process has begun. I don't know where it will take me. Sometimes it is fun; sometimes it is painful to rake up these long hidden, but not forgotten, experiences. But the door has been opened and there is no going back.

Coming to
America

I was ten years old when my sister Bea and I were told that we were going to live with our Bubby and Zaida, our grandmother and grandfather. We were now orphans. Our father had just died. Bea, two years older than I, knew who these people were but I didn't. I was eighteen months old when our mother died. A marriage was arranged for my father a year or so later. Apparently my grandparents thought it was better for us to live like a "normal" family, without my mother's ghost hovering around. Previously, we rarely saw this grandmother of mine, and I had no idea who she was. When she visited me, she was always laden with gifts and food. A few times that I can recall, my father took Bea and me to her grocery store and we were allowed to take any sweets that tempted us. When I asked who she was, I was told, "a relative."

We were such hungry children, Bea and I, both literally and emotionally. Now food was plentiful for we two skinny, underfed kids, but emotional sustenance was neither understood nor taken into account. Zaida was sweet but Bubby, the powerhouse in the family, was cold. She held us at arm's length. It was not until I became a parent that I understood the fence that Bubby had built around herself. What I was able to put together was that my mother, her firstborn, died at twenty-nine, never having fully recovered after my birth and she shut down. The struggle of my family's seven year journey to America took its toll and this was the last straw.

Nobody wanted to talk about it. They were just so grateful to be here and wanted to survive and get on with their lives. All I knew was that she ran the grocery store with two of her sons, had charity boxes all around the kitchen, was the president of the Ladies Auxiliary of her synagogue, and was known as the Sage of Blake Avenue. In Brooklyn, whoever had a problem and needed advice knew that on a Sunday afternoon, he or she could come see to Mrs. Weinstein, have a glass of tea, and she would help them figure out what to do. She was a big fan of the radio program, "The Yiddish Filosof," the Jewish Philosopher which, combined with her native intelligence, made her a cut above the rest. Bubby was a very respected part of the community in her own. The fact that she took in two orphans made her even larger than life, but I was too young to understand.

My quests to really get to know my Bubby came late in her life when she started spending summers in my home. She finally would open up a little and talk about hidden pain. She died with dignity at ninety-four.

They always knew that one day they would have to leave, but this shtettle in Belorussia was their home. All of their predecessors were buried there and how does one leave the family home, the granary, and the business that provided funds for all of the younger siblings to go to America? Once there, what would they do? They wouldn't starve; the whole family was there, but a businessman in his fifties did not want or expect his family to take care of him and his children. It was better to stay put for a while longer and see what happened. And then it did. The pogroms burst out in full force. The Cossacks came roaring into the town on their horses and everyone was fair game to be stomped upon. Death to the Jews was the order of the day. No, the days and nights. Anyone in sight, male or female, young or old, was a perfect foil for these "heroes" of Czarist Russia, the elite, the Cossacks. They rejoiced in their boisterous uncivilized behavior and bragged of their disgraceful achievements which they carried on with impunity. This was not the first pogrom for the gentle Weinstein family, but it was their last.

Children were taught to always be on the alert for the sound of horses, and they are taught to come home immediately from where they were. If they were too far away, they were to hide in the woods until things quieted down. Norman was ten years old and was playing near the home of some friends when the Cossacks came tearing into the village.

"Run for your lives!" they all shouted and ran in different directions. As he approached the road to his house, he saw that it was too late. So he ran into the woods and hid. As darkness approached, he realized that the soldiers were drunk and on a killing spree. His only hope for survival was to stay hidden in the woods. Cold and hungry, he covered himself with some branches and cried himself to sleep. The rampage went on for three days and finally the satiated drunken Cossacks left. The terrified ten year old crawled and stumbled home to his hysterical parents and siblings and the decision was made: "Now is the time to go to America."

Once the decision was made, the difficulties that would confront them surfaced. It would take two years to get everything organized. Travel arrangements were complicated. The least of their problems was dealing with their belongings, but it was a problem nonetheless. Everything that they wanted to take would have to be shipped to Hamburg and of course, the choice was very limited.

This could and would be accomplished. There were many eager outstretched hands anxious to get Papa Wolf's granary, and that problem was disposed of. Travel passes had to be gotten: not too easy a task, but silver crossed palms and so it was achieved.

The biggest problem was fear of the trip itself, the trip to Hamburg. Many roads would have to be traversed, many towns would have to be passed through, and Jews were extremely unpopular. Times in Russia were turbulent: two percent of the people owned 98 percent of the wealth under the Czar and a convenient scapegoat, as usual was "The Jew." The Jew was very obvious because of their difference in dress and general difference in appearance. Jews were not allowed to own land so Jewish men were not farmers. They did not have the ruddy skin, large muscled bodies and rough hands that distinguished farmers from scholars or businessmen. They would have to disguise themselves for the journey.

Fortunately, Papa Wolf was a large man and forged a plan. He was friendly with some of his customers who brought their wheat to the granary for processing. He arranged for two wagons of hay to transport them. He would dress up like a farmer, no typical Orthodox clothing, no black hat, the yarmulke hidden under a cap. He would drive one cart with Mama Frieda next to him dressed similarly as a farmer's wife. The farmer would drive the other cart and the seven children would be hidden under the hay whenever they approached a village or a town. It was a plan.

Then there were the children. The oldest was Yentl, or Henrietta. She was nineteen at the onset of the trip. Then the brothers, Morris, Sam, David, Norman, sister Sadie, and baby Harry, not quite three years old. Quite a handful to deal with but Frodel, or Frieda, would handle that end if it. The difficulties were foreseeable and would be dealt with. What came next was unforeseeable. They arrived in a Jewish village in the Ukraine called Yampol and decided to rest for a day or so. That day or so turned out to be four years. World War One broke out and they were stuck in Yampol for the duration.

Yampol was a village fairly well known to Papa Wolf. He had spent some years there in his youth and he knew some people and people knew him, making it possible for him to conduct some business and support his family. Frieda put her baking skills to work, opening a bread bakery and so the transition was not too difficult. Henrietta became a beautiful young woman and was pursued by many of the young men in Yampol.

However, when Louis Lieberman returned from the Russian Army, dashing and handsome in his uniform, the competition was over. He was for her and she was for him. He was an intellectual and his father, a comfortable land broker, encouraged him to pursue his intellectual interests. Louis' older sister Lena was already married to a rich Texas businessman in Corpus Christi, his older brother Isaac was settled in Boston with his family, and his younger sister Sonia was a pharmacist interning in the local pharmacy. Louis was the apple of his parents, Bertha and Simon's eye, and the marriage of Henrietta to Louis was celebrated by both sets of parents.

Laws in Russia at that time were very contradictory. A Jew was not allowed to own land, but a Jew could appraise the value of land and broker sales between non-Jews. And so this too was a family that was financially comfortable, and yet could not own a home.

Life settled into a pattern and in November of 1918, the war ended and motion started again to bring the Weinstein family to America. Papers were once again secured, arrangements were again made, and the family was on their journey. This time the destination was Danzig, a free state in the German free corridor, now known as Gdansk, Poland. This was the major port of debarkation from Eastern Europe. Again the trip was arduous and by the time the family arrived in Danzig, Henrietta was pregnant. The excitement of finally being on the cusp of getting to America was more than one could imagine. As the family finally started boarding the ship, papers in hand, Henrietta was asked to step aside.

"You are pregnant, miss?" the guard asked.

"Yes, of course," she replied. "Why do you ask? This is my husband and my family. Is there a problem? I have my papers and my ticket."

"You cannot board this ship. You will have to remain here until your baby is born."

He was adamant. Although Frieda and Wolf were shattered, having been told that they could not take the children aboard the ship or they would forfeit their assigned space, they broken heartedly boarded the ship. They had been assured that Henrietta and Louis would be able to continue on to the United States after the baby was born.

When the family debarked at Ellis Island, everyone passed through customs and then went on to health inspection. Six year old Harry had chicken pox and had to be quarantined; another heart breaking decision for Frieda. Her older child was left in Danzig and now her youngest on Ellis Island. She decided to stay with Harry, and Wolf continued on with the rest of the children to meet the family in New York. It took two long weary weeks and finally they were reunited with their family in Williamsburg, Brooklyn, New York.

On January 7th, 1921, a baby girl was born to Henrietta and Louis in Danzig. When this daughter, Bela was three months old, they arrived at Ellis Island, and went on to Williamsburg. Suffice it to say, the family was overjoyed and it became time for the young couple to make a life for themselves. But, what was Louis to do with his intellectualism and no job training? They lived with Mama Frieda and Papa Wolf, and Louis helped in the grocery store which the Weinstein's had acquired. The difficult trip had taken its toll on Henrietta and when a second daughter was born not quite two years later, Henrietta remained quite frail.

Eighteen months had passed and her life had ended. The family was devastated and Louis was bereft. After a year of mourning, it was decided that Louis needed a wife, the girls needed a mother, and life had to go on. A marriage was arranged with a young widow from Boston who had a daughter two years older than Bela. It was obvious that if this arrangement were to take on a semblance of normalcy, the young family had to move to their own home and Louis had to find work elsewhere.

It is quite sad to report that this lovely man, like so many others who could not yet speak the language, was forced to take work far beneath his station and intelligence, but he had to make a living for his family, and what a family it was.

Irwin was born and now there were three girls and a boy. It would be nice to say that Helen was an ideal mother and stepmother, but that would be an exaggeration. She got high marks as a mother to her children, but she was a stereotypical stepmother. Though not physically abusive, with one word and look she could send the two sisters cowering. They were terrified of her. Bela, the older sister, understood that this mother was not a real mother. Esther, the younger sister, was still a baby when the marriage took place and labored under the illusion that this was a real mother-father and children family, although she sometimes wondered.

One day when she was older, she told her friend that she didn't think *that* mama was her *real* mother. Her friend crossed herself and said it was a sin to think such a thing, and so the subject never came up again.

Times had become very bad. Food was sometimes scarce and Louis had very severe asthma, which developed into tuberculosis from which he eventually died at the age of forty-four. Bela and Esther had to make regular visits to the Jewish hospital for periodic chest x-rays. It was not clear why only the two girls were involved.

Louis spent the last months of his life at the Montifiore

Hospital in the Bronx, a very long train ride from Brooklyn where his wife and children lived. Several times Helen took the two girls to visit him. There was a fruit stand at the base of the elevated train station and they would buy two oranges to bring him as a gift. There was barely enough money to take the train, let alone a gift of greater consequence.

Louis understood full well that he was dying and his tortured concern was for his two motherless daughters. One Saturday, when he realized that the end was very near, he called one of Frieda's sons and asked him to bring Frieda to the hospital. He knew that Frieda was an Orthodox Jew who never rode on the Sabbath, but also knew that if he asked her to come that she would understand the urgency and oblige.

When she came to his bedside, he could barely speak. He gathered his strength and whispered to her, "Promise me that you will take care of my girls." And then, he died.

The Military Lifestyle

Most nice Jewish girls did not follow their husbands and take up residence near army camps. Most nice Jewish girls stayed home with their mother or mother-in-law. But that was not the case for me. I look back at that girl and wonder where the courage came from. Maybe it was naivety, or maybe it was foolishness, or even ignorance. Whatever it was, it took courage and the experience was priceless. Very few of my contemporaries in our poor immigrant neighborhood went to college. We educated ourselves in that special academy, the college of hard knocks. And traveling around in the heartland of our country was a priceless education.

I had never been anywhere. Out of town was New Jersey

and I had never even been there. There I was at Grand Central Station, dressed up in a little pale blue suit with matching hat, carrying my beautiful white trimmed alligator luggage. Grand Central Station in New York was and still is awesome, and I was awestruck as I boarded the train to Chicago where I would change trains and get the train to Kansas.

I found a window seat quickly, and two sailors sat down, one alongside and one opposite me. They were headed to San Diego and would be on the same Kansas bound train after Chicago. I must say it was fortuitous because, being the gentlemen that they were, they carried my luggage for me. I admit that the conversation between the three of us could have been construed as flirtatious during the three-day trip, sitting up day and night. But as I said they were gentlemen, and it certainly helped pass the time. Upon, arriving in Junction City, I felt like I could have been a movie star. Two cute sailors got off with me, carrying the luggage and there was my handsome husband, and handsome he was, with his buddy Jim waiting to receive me.

It was early April, and spring in small town USA is quite different from spring in Brooklyn, New York. Sixty years later, I remember being struck by the way the air in the early evening felt palpable. I felt like I could almost hold it in my hands along with the scent of honeysuckles, or maybe it was lilacs. I was barely twenty, carefree, and I was in love. My husband had rented a room for me in the home of a pleasant woman. It was actually her living room with a few scant pieces of furniture and a double bed stuck in the middle of the room. It had French doors that were discreetly covered with curtains, which gave us a modicum of privacy. I was allowed to keep one or two items in the refrigerator and I had a one burner hot plate and one pot.

Que had a pass which allowed him off camp several nights a week if they were not on maneuvers. Sardines, salami or salmon from Bubby's packages, along with canned soup and bread, sustained us during the months he was at Fort Riley, Kansas. We did eat a real meal once a week in a place called The Pig Trail Inn. It cost $2.50 for the two of us. That was as much as we could afford on a Corporal's pay.

Shortly after arrival, I sought out the Jewish USO funded by the National Jewish Welfare Board. I met four other women native to New York, Connecticut, and Virginia, and we became fast friends. Nobody would hire wives of soldiers in the 4th Armored Division because it was common knowledge that they would be shipping out, so work was unavailable to us. Instead we spent the days playing Chinese checkers, developing film and printing pictures, seeing the occasional movie, or just hanging around talking and learning from each other.

As a matter of fact one of the girls, we were little more than girls at that time, changed the course of my sex life. She educated me about the Margaret Sanger clinic in New York where one could go and be fitted for a diaphragm! I must admit that although I was married for several weeks at that time, I knew nothing about my body. Nice Jewish girls knew that a boy, even if engaged to him, was not allowed to touch your breasts. Well maybe, but surely not below the waist. Then somehow magically on your wedding night, you were supposed to get into bed, spread your legs, become deflowered and enjoy sex.

Well it just didn't happen that way and the boys that were married did not know much more than we did. We had to grow into a satisfying conjugal experience. Among those of us at that USO there was one older, more experienced girl. She told us about the Margaret Sanger Clinic. On my first return to New York that's exactly what I did. Putting that experience in the context of the times, it was quite a risky and avant-garde thing to do, and since we were definitely not going to have a baby while the war was going on and he was going to go overseas at any time, that decision made my husband very happy.

At that time, I did not want to become pregnant, and I certainly did not want my husband to either use a condom or practice *coitus interruptus*. It seems ridiculous now that condoms are advertised in movie houses and on television, and dispensed in machines in high schools. But in those days, they were sold surreptitiously behind the counter in the back of the pharmacy, and never in the presence of a female. For a woman to be in charge of birth control was very avant-garde, and I decided it was for me. Our next furlough was my opportunity.

With the address secreted away in my wallet, I took the train into lower Manhattan. I was pretty nervous when I knocked as instructed on the door of a basement apartment of a rather seedy old building. I was admitted by a smiling youngish woman dressed as a nurse, and found myself surrounded by women in their twenties and thirties, all appearing a bit skittish. I almost left, but calmed down and took a seat. When my name was called, my determination overcame by trepidations and I met the wonderful Margaret Sanger.

She was kind of bookish looking, and sort of old fashioned. She didn't look anything like a sex specialist. Intuiting my discomfort, she took my hands and gave me a big smile. With her arm around my shoulder she gave me a flawless description of the female body and its capacity for pleasure in intimacy. I did not realize how ignorant I was in that area and my head was spinning with all of this new information. She fitted me with a diaphragm, taught me how to use it and how to examine it to make sure it was perfect. Her advice to me was to use it nightly and always be prepared. I thanked her, paid the fee, and left.

Although the clinic was not exactly illegal, it was frowned upon by the medical profession. Eventually the system came around and OB/GYNs started dispensing contraceptives for women. But for me, sneaking around to that seedy clinic on the lower East Side was an unforgettable experience. It did change my sex life radically and my diaphragm was affectionately dubbed Margaret.

If you've ever driven through Kansas you know that it is flat and boring. Life in Kansas, for me, was also flat and boring but I wanted to be with my husband. However, after a few months, the picture changed. The Ninth Armored Engineers were being transferred to the Mojave Desert in Southern California and we five Eastern girls were going to Los Angeles. I was going to be near family. My stepmother, my stepsister Marcia, and my half-brother Irwin lived near there. When I called to tell them of the forthcoming change, Marcia immediately invited me to stay with her. She had a pullout couch and I was welcome for as long as I wanted. She also assured me that she and her mother could and would find small, furnished apartments for the other wives. L.A. was very transient and furnished apartments were bountiful. Problem solved.

Getting to California was another story. The flight from Kansas was about two hours. The train trip from Junction City to Los Angeles took three days. Flying at that time was not an option. Commercial flights were nonexistent. The military needed the meager amount of planes to transport military personnel, but not the troops. They went by troop train. Good portions of civilian trains were likewise commandeered for military purposes. During World War II everybody understood that we were at war and had to deal with all of the accompanying inconveniences.

When the train arrived we boarded, but we were dismayed to find it very full. We were fortunate to find one bank of two seats, but that was it. We parked the largest of our suitcase alongside the seat that we had. Two of us sat in the seats. Clara, who was pregnant, got to sit the whole time, while the rest of us rotated. There were five of us, so two sat in the seats, two sat on the suitcase leaning against the seat and the fifth one roamed the train.

This train was fairly modern for the times, and the floors of the Ladies rooms were large and carpeted. They would have been comfortable to sit on but women with babies, of which there were many, preempted us. This leg of the journey took us to Denver where we had to change trains.

Seeing Denver from the railroad station on a beautiful June morning in 1943 was truly a magnificent sight. This small city nestled against the majesty of the snowcapped Rocky Mountains was breathtaking, and is something one never forgets. It looked to me like pictures I had seen of

Switzerland. After the flatlands of Kansas, I oozed excitement over this, but we never left the train station. We used the facilities and were happy to be able to sit quietly, all together, on the benches until the next train came.

Again the train was quite full and we ran, lugging our suitcases, from train to train. We ended up in the first car and were able to find seats. Actually that car was relatively empty when we got to it, so we grabbed double seats so as to be together, and eventually the seats filled up and the train got moving. We were thrilled with our good fortune. Not only did we have seats but they were also plush green velvet. What we didn't know was that this train had a coal driven engine which sent a steady stream of dense black smoke back into the open windows of the first car. We were also surprised when a conductor came in at dusk with a ladder and proceeded to light the gas lamps on the ceiling of the train.

I managed to sleep a little and when we got to Salt Lake City in the morning, skin and clothing were black and filthy from the exposure to the coal dust and smoke. Fortunately, someone had given us the address of a woman who, in an effort to support the war, was kind enough to offer army wives a place to clean up and rest for a few hours between trains for a very small sum. We gratefully took advantage of the opportunity to bathe and rest until the last leg of the trip. This portion was more civilized and we finally arrived in sunny, clean, pastel Union Station, Los Angeles, California.

Summer in L.A. gets pretty hot and I drifted through the next few months. Although I did feel well protected being with my family, my major occupation was worrying. The war was revving up on all fronts and Que's battalion was getting desert training. Did that mean North Africa where war was raging against Mussolini's Italian army? Where was North Africa and what did that have to do with Europe. We civilians were so ill informed. The only thing we knew was to worry, and I was and still am an expert in that arena.

It was hard to know whether or not Que was worried or afraid. The Bogen men prided themselves in their macho approach to life. I always knew it was a façade behind which he could hide his real feelings and I was not going to deflate his protective bubble.

Being the only Jew in his unit, he needed to present a very strong and confident persona although in reality he was a very gentle, sweet man, who was barely more than a boy. He was 22 years old, and the army was a process of evolution. Boys trained hard, became men, and were then sent into action to kill or be killed.

Once in a while, Que would get a rare and much coveted weekend pass. He would hitch rides with some army vehicle and we would have a day and a half with each other. Marcia's husband, Boxer, was sensitive to the fact that we needed some time alone besides being intimate on the pullout couch, and would lend us his prized 1940 Buick.

It would be quite a few years before cars started being built again. Everything that was civilian screeched to a halt on 12/7/41, and converted to the needs of the military, and so a fairly new car and some time alone was truly precious. We would drive up into the Hollywood Hills, contemplate the spectacular views, and dream about one day being free of the war, being ordinary people who lived ordinary lives. We were, after all, very ordinary people when we became engaged a year and a half before we got married.

That was such a special night, our engagement night. Bubby and Zaida were celebrating their 50th anniversary and a big "affair" was to take place. Zaida was a revered member of the Synagogue congregation and as such, it was customary to invite another member of consequence to your celebration. When I learned that Que's parents were invited, it did not faze me because Mr. Bogen footed the bill. I was sick in bed with la grippe, now called the flu, but of course I was going to the party. Que picked me up, drove to his home to get his parents, and presented me with a ring. My sister, Bea, had become engaged a few weeks before and so that night was a night of celebration for us all.

It would be a few years before celebrations of that nature could take place again. The next one was New Year's Eve of 1945. The war had ended in August and Que set foot in the United States on that evening.

During the war, it was not uncommon for the military to move around without advance information and suddenly the 9th Armored was evacuated from the Mojave Desert to an unknown destination and it was time for me to go home. The problem was, I had no home. My sister and husband had moved in with Bubby and Zaida, occupying our room, so I went to live with Aunt Sadie … the living room couch became my bed. Que had been transferred to Camp Polk, Louisiana and after a few months, he got furlough and came to get me.

Traveling in the South in 1944 was an unforgettable experience. My husband knew me; he knew that I was outspoken, and so he forewarned me that I would see things that I had never seen before, and that I had to realize that there was nothing, *nothing* that I could do about it. In other words, he was warning me to keep my mouth shut. When we changed trains in Washington, D.C., I got the picture.

Lavatories and drinking fountains were labeled "Colored." I had heard that this existed but in the capital of our country? Yes, in the capital of our country. Que was right. He knew that I would be shocked, and shocked I was!

We finally arrived in Shreveport where we would take a four hour bus trip to Leesville, which is a small town close to the camp. We arrived at the bus depot which was teeming with soldiers. It was Sunday evening, and most of these soldiers had to be back in camp for roll call in the morning.

There was a dispatcher who loaded up the buses and who shouted, "All right, now. Six niggers, and the rest white."

Six niggers and the rest white? These were soldiers in uniform preparing to fight for our country overseas, to get killed, or worse yet, terribly maimed, and still they weren't good enough to sit anywhere but the last six seats in the back of the bus.

Que did not have to return to camp until Tuesday and I told him that I would not get on the bus, which by now was leaving with empty seats while the black soldiers hung around. Another young woman we had met on the train felt as I did. Her husband had to get back to camp so the three of us sat in the bus station all night. Rather, we slept on the benches and in the morning, everyone was gone and we went on to Leesville. My education about prejudice had only just begun.

If you come from up North and you have never traveled down South before Rosa Parks and Martin Luther King, and before Linden B. Johnson liberated the Negroes, as they were then called, then you would be just as ignorant and shocked as I was at the attitude and language that prevailed. There was no restraint or self-consciousness about using what we now refer to as the "N" word because in Louisiana the "N's" were considered inferior people to be used as maids or workers. They were barely tolerated and the attitude toward the Jews was not much better.

Que had made arrangements for a room in a pastor's home for four days during which time I was to find a more permanent place. He had taken a fair sized room and boxed it off into four cubbies, each of which had a bed against the wall, a chair, and a nightstand. There wasn't room for anything else. The makeshift wall was about six feet high and the ceiling was about eight feet high, making the two top feet of the four cubbies kind of community space. Under those conditions, if anyone farted everyone shared in the scent and if anyone had an orgasm everyone shared in ecstasy. For this accommodation we had the privilege of paying $2.50 a night, which was about double what we could afford to pay on the $50.00 a month that I received and the $21.00 a month that Que got. One portion of his GI pay was sent to his mother.

There was one bathroom that had two doors with another such arrangement on the other side of the second door, and whose walls were decorated with all kind of signs, such as "Don't leave hair in the sink" or "Don't throw condoms in the toilet" and most importantly "Don't forget to unlock the door when you leave!" Imagine the chaos if one forgot to unlock the door to the other side and all four GI's or their wives were locked out? Luckily that didn't happen when I was here.

Day two after night one I set out on my quest to find

a room. The streets in Leesville were not paved and at each corner there were three steps down to the road. This was Bayou country and in the mornings there was dense fog which rose from the ground up and almost dissipated for the most part during the course of the day. Fog rising from unpaved roads translated into plain old mud, and I was down to one pair of shoes. They were brown pumps and the heels would sink into the damned mud, which made crossing streets a big challenge.

I trudged up and down those God forsaken miserable streets and knocked at every door that had a For Rent sign on it. The lady of the house, and I use that term loosely, would open the door, hear my New York accent asking about the room, look at my dark hair and Jewish face and slam the door. I didn't get it at first but by day four, I did get it and I was desperate.

I was sitting in the USO, quietly crying as I absorbed the fact that nobody was going to rent a room to Jewish girl from New York and I would have to go back to New York the next day when a softly accented Southern voice said to me, "Esther honey, is that you?" Elsie Lipshitz from Virginia, one of my Kansas/California friends was here in Leesville and she immediately came to my rescue.

She and another friend, Clara Tinter, were both living in a house that had three rooms let out to army wives. The third girl was leaving the next day because her husband had shipped out, and Elsie was sure that she could get the room for me, which she did. A whole new episode in my life was about to unfurl.

Our landlady, Mrs. Martin, was a forty or fifty something schoolteacher. She and her mom occupied the lower level of the house. How she taught children, I never knew, because her command of the English language was pathetic by New York standards, but a teacher she was. She would storm into the house after work, put up a pot of very strong coffee, take off her shoes, sit down on a chair on the porch, put her feet up on the rail with a cigarette in mouth, and guzzle her coffee. After an hour or so of this ritual, she would cook some kind of gumbo for dinner.

The kitchen was a place to be avoided. I would turn on the light and watch with horror the parade of water bugs and humongous cockroaches, the likes of which I never knew existed. Now, I was not a white gloved princess who never saw roaches. I was a Brooklyn girl from East New York–

not the slums but not exactly the Upper East Side—but these roaches were ominous. They were to be avoided at all costs, and so we did.

Life was hot, humid, and lazy. This was an absolutely intellectual desert; there was no place to go, nothing to see, and nothing to do. Days were so boring that one day when Mrs. Martin started painting the spokes on the porch railing, we all grabbed brushes and pitched in.

The radio was suddenly interrupted by a news broadcast relating that it was D-day and the Yanks had landed. The Americans had stormed Omaha Beach, Normandy. We were savvy enough, we army wives, to understand that this European push meant that our husbands would probably be expedited and perhaps would be the beginning of the end of this dreadful experience. Maybe by the time they got overseas it would all be over and life would return back to normal.

Leesville, Louisiana was a real experience in culture shock, some of which was blatantly visible. It was indeed shocking to see many men with one arm and half of another, having lost part of a limb in the lumber mill or in the process of cutting down trees. These men would be hanging around town or walking around listlessly. They were, after all, unemployed and abandoned by their employers. They were worthless.

Another astonishing thing was the slowness with which everything moved, particularly in speech. It created the impression that general intelligence was pretty low, but that was only an impression. Many of these people were, in fact, well educated, to wit my landlady Mrs. Martin, the schoolteacher.

One day she stopped me as I was about to go up to my room and said to me, "Esser honey, how come yo daddy married up wif a Jewish girl?"

Que Bogen surely did not have a Jewish name and he really was Teutonic looking, and so her assumption was understandable.

I responded to her, "My daddy is Jewish."

Astonished, she replied, "Really? I never would have thought so."

The door was opened so I took the risk of asking her what they all had against Jews. "I don't know," she answered. "We don't know many Jews. There is only one Jew in town. We don't even know his name. Everyone calls him The Jew, and he owns the Silver Dollar Café."

I thought back to my frightened days only a few months before, trudging through the muddy streets of Leesville trying to find a place to stay while my husband was preparing to go overseas and having doors shut in my face because I was a New York Jew. How did they know? Olive skin, dark hair, prominent nose, and a Northern accent, that was how they knew.

After D-Day, things really intensified for the troops. Field trips and maneuvers were longer, nights off base were fewer and most weekend passes were cancelled. In the midst of all of this I got really sick. I had been subject to very bad tonsillitis and no amount of swabbing with iodine could deal with the abscesses. Que took me to the army hospital; they took one look in my throat and issued an emergency furlough for him to take me home for surgery. They would not touch me, so we went off to New York. I fully expected to return to Leesville and left my footlocker with most of my stuff in my room. When I said goodbye to Mrs. Martin, she shed a few tears and told me that if I didn't come back she would rent her rooms only to Jewish girls because nobody else in town would. As it turned out, I never returned.

The only regret I had about not returning to Louisiana was never getting to New Orleans. Que really wanted to go and so we wrote home to his mother to send us $100.00 of our money. We had about $300.00 left to our names, the last remnants of our wedding gifts. His mother sent us a letter via his sister, telling us that she is his mother, and therefore had a right to say that she does not see any reason to go to New Orleans and that we should not spend our money so foolishly, ignorant woman that she was. Her son was prepping to go overseas, to be in combat, to perhaps be killed or maimed and she denied him this pleasure. Well, of course when I got home to my grandparents', I borrowed $100.00 from my grandmother and sent it to him. He managed to get a pass and go, and I was happy for him.

The tonsillectomy was a nightmare that I would not rather discuss, but it is permanently inscribed in my memory as one of the worst experiences in my life. After three weeks when I still could not speak, my footlocker was sent home and Que was transferred to Fort Dix, New Jersey. He came home to me in the evening and his brother picked him up at 5 a.m. to get him to a train back to Ft. Dix. This happened three days in a row, and on the third night we never went to bed. We just sat up all night in my grandmother's kitchen and talked until dawn broke and it was time for him to go. Que smoked in those days, Camels unfiltered. I took the stub of his cigarette and put it into my wedding ring box and I did not see him again for a year and a half.

That night, Que came home from Ft. Dix had an eerie feeling about it, but then again nothing was certain in those days. Everything was kind of play acting, always waiting for the curtain to fall, but on what? It was like a rehearsal for a play, but nobody had the script. We couldn't possibly know what to expect. The war was raging, and there was absolutely no communication other than letters which took two weeks to pass through censors and arrive home; most of the information was obliterated for security reasons.

Of necessity, life took on a pattern. I went back to my job in the office of a defense company. Many of the women were married to service people overseas and we clung to each other for any kind of socialization that we allowed ourselves; the occasional dinner or perhaps a movie, but not too often. In order to hold on to their workforce, this company offered a two week vacation to all employees, factory workers and all, paid in full at a hotel in the Catskills called, the Emerson.

It was very nice, but not for those of us who had seen a bit of life.

We elected to go to a place called Green Mansions on Schroon Lake in the Adirondacks, and it was a great relief from the stress of being an army wife with a husband overseas. There was even a bit of romantic undertone with an attractive vacationing civilian government employee, but conscience ruled over desire so there is no point in exploring that issue. However if it becomes relevant, I can visit it again.

Every week I sent a package to Que, consisting of a variety of things such as salami, some cans of salmon or tuna, cigarettes of course, and the main item. I would get a loaf of rye bread from the bakery, cut it in half, scoop out the innards, insert a small bottle of rye whiskey, close it and wrap it, the main item! He loved those packages, the few that he actually got. Some of my friends scoffed at me for sending those weekly packages because realistically most of them went astray, but my feelings were if one of those got to him, it was more than none, and so those packages went out weekly.

It is very hard to share the emotions of that period of time, the constant nagging fear that insinuated itself into everything said and done. How can anyone living in the twenty-first century, the time of cell phones and computers, Skype and iPods, and all of the other electronics that we take for granted, understand that there was absolutely no way of getting in touch? To know what was happening to yours, you read the papers three days later, you went to the movies and maybe, just maybe there would be a film in the news that related to your loved one. I don't minimize the fear or stress that military families endure these days, and if they pay a price, the price is real. However those days, weeks, and months of no contact were hell.

I was living with my grandparents in an apartment on the first floor. The entrance into the lower floor had a squeaky door. We could hear it from the kitchen and when I would hear that door squeak sometimes in the evening, I was always sure that it was a telegram, coming to tell me that I was no longer a wife, that at twenty-two, I was a widow. It didn't happen that way, but I was always a really good worrier, and I did until it ended and he came home.

Ordinary language in the 1940s did not include words like agoraphobia. In fact most general practitioners were not acquainted with phobias of any type and had no clue about what to do about one if in fact they did recognize it. Nor did they understand what a panic attack was and how it could be handled. Psychiatrists were few and far between and certainly not in the part of Brooklyn in which I lived and so when I started having panic attacks accompanied by agoraphobia I thought that I was having a heart attack and would die. I was all of twenty-two years old when it started.

The war was at its height and Que was in the thick of it. My best friend Minnie, who was young like me and worked in the same office as I did, had become a widow. Her husband, who had been in the same field of operation as mine, had been mowed down in the Ardennes Forest, which added greatly to the fear and stress of everyday living. My life had assumed a pattern of its own. I would come home from work and go straight to the grocery store. There was a kitchen in the back and Bubby would make dinner of some sort for me, after which we would go up to our apartment. There, after searching the newspaper for any news of the 9th Armored Division I would busy myself writing letters to Que.

One night I came home and she wasn't in the store. My Uncle Sam told me that she wasn't feeling well, that she was at home, and that the doctor was there. I rushed upstairs and as I walked into her room the doctor shoved a glass bottle of blood into my hand and told me to hold it higher than my head. It was attached to a tube and he was transfusing her. That scene was too much for me to absorb and I told the doctor that I was feeling faint.

"Get that torch lamp," he shouted at me and he hung the bottle of blood on the lamp. I don't know whether or not I actually fainted but I did have to put my head between my knees until I could function again.

Bubby had bleeding ulcers and she was having a real serious incident. The ulcers slowly healed but she remained ill and her skin turned yellow. Her eyes looked like egg yolks. The doctor ordered whatever tests were available and he diagnosed stomach cancer. She was seventy-five years old and as sharp as anyone twenty years younger. My sister's husband would not accept that deadly diagnosis and took her to a special diagnostic clinic in New York, which was a very big deal at that time. There they diagnosed gall stones that had gotten into the tubes leading into her gallbladder causing her to turn yellow, she underwent successful surgery, recovered slowly, went back to work in the store part time and died at ninety-four. This experience took a very heavy toll on me, although I did not understand it at the time when I experienced my first panic attack.

It is masochistic to resurrect the details of a panic attack and the desolation of agoraphobia. As someone who is not a masochist in the interest of self-preservation, I will only offer insight into this kind of agony very briefly.

Bubby had survived the surgery, was still yellow and was far from well. She also had extreme itching of her skin and could only find relief in a warm oatmeal bath. Her daughter, my aunt Sadie, was in attendance by day and I was around at night and weekends. I vaguely recall that some of the time there was outside help. Between the situation at home and the devastating news about the war, life was very grim, to say the least. The Germans had gained a great advantage and had surrounded the Allied armies in the infamous Battle of the Bulge which started on December 15, 1944, my twenty-second birthday, and lasted for several weeks, during the coldest spell in Belgium's history. Thousands of Americans were killed or maimed, and we at home were clueless. All we knew from news reports was the bits and pieces about the different units that were involved, and whatever we heard during those weeks was bad, very bad. The war was to continue until May of 1945, but that period was surely the darkest of the conflagration for the U.S.

One evening I was coming home from work on the train when suddenly I started to sweat profusely, began to tremble, felt faint and at the same time felt my heart pounding in my chest and ears. I was sure that my time had come, like my mother who had died so young. I wanted to scream and to make the train stop so that I could get off. I started to talk some kind of nonsense to a man sitting near me and he innocently distracted me in conversation until the train arrived at my station and I could run off.

I really could not deal with my ailing grandmother, but I had to and as my claustrophobia deepened it became more and more difficult to ride on the train. Panic attacks were lurking nearby all of the time. It finally reached a point when I needed a respite and my sister-in-law Teddy came to the rescue, temporarily. I stayed with her for a few days during which time she took me to see a doctor.

He was a regular family physician but had an interest in and was taking courses in Psychiatry. He explained to me that since I had experienced so much loss and death as a child, losing my mother when I was an infant, the discovery that my mother was my stepmother and the subsequent breakup of our family when my father died when I was ten, and now my grandmother, the iron rod, the bulwark had clay feet and was flirting with death–this was all too much for me. He also explained that the train, particularly as it went underground or through a tunnel, which was the most frightening, represented the grave to me and gave me cause to panic.

It is emotionally draining to tell about this and although my panic attacks have been at bay these many years, the scars remain and perhaps it is wise not to scratch the surface too deeply.

Que's letters, for which I was so hungry, were the focus of my life. They would arrive sporadically, a few at a time. They were love letters. Anything that could be construed as information would be censored out. The sweetness and declarations of love and loneliness were enough to nourish and satisfy me. I would read and reread them repeatedly, my tears of heartsickness blurring the words and staining the pages, sometimes washing the words off.

There were periods of time when as much as three weeks

would go by without a word, no communication whatsoever. We at home had no information except headlines in the newspaper or Pathé news in the movie houses, and the news was generally foreboding, to say the least. After a while there would be a breakthrough and mail would come trickling through. At least I would know that on the date of the last letter he was alive and okay. The war was very intense. He was all of twenty-three years old.

My Darling,

Mail call was wonderful today. I got a bunch of your letters. Probably some of them got lost. I also got mail from Mom and other family members. I kept yours, as I always do, for last. I have enough of them to read over and over and they comfort me to know that you miss me as much as I miss you. It means more to me than anything else in the world. I want you not to worry about me. I survived this huge _____ with nothing more than _____ feet in spite of the freezing weather. It was so good to get a change of socks and to be able to put my damp socks under my arms so they won't freeze. We learn all kinds of _____ of survival here.

Among my family mail was a letter from my sister Ettie. She asked me to pray that they don't send her husband Milty, the MP in the States overseas. Is she nuts? I don't care if they dig up my father and send him to replace me so that I can come home to you. How I miss you, my darling wife, the love of my life.

Que

April 20, 1945 Somewhere in ------------------------

My darling moonflower:

Although my heart aches for you it is now filled with some hope. I cannot wait to hold you in my arms again. It is 8 long months since ------- -------- ----- ------------, but now that the Germans -------- ----- ----------- ------- --- looking forward to coming home to you and a good long rest.

Your package came yesterday and Mileo, O'Donnel and I had a party. Nowicki couldn't join us because he took a small ------------- -- - ---- ---- -----. Not good enough to send him home but at least he's sleeping on a cot, not like -------------- -------- ----------- --------.

Have to go now…all my love always,
Que.

Although the war in Europe ended in May and in the Pacific in August, the troops did not start coming home for a few months. Injured servicemen came home first, followed by married men with children, and then came the married men without children, and finally the single men. They had a point system: twelve points for each category. Que fell into the third category, and so the wait continued. The much awaited telegram came on December 26, 1945. It was dated the day before, and it read: *DARLING LOADING FROM LE HAVRE DEC 26 BE WITH YOU SOON LOVE QUE.* Just like that, those words, and my life, were about to change.

I had no way of knowing when he would actually arrive and the anticipation was intense. Had he changed? Had I changed? After all of the worrying and angst would I still be pretty in his eyes? Had he fallen in love with someone else while stationed in Germany? I had a good reason to ask that.

His buddy, Jim Mileo, came home several weeks earlier and he came to see me. I always knew, during the time I spent with the army, that Jim had a crush on me. He would hang around like an adoring puppy, and Que would kid him about it. Neither one of us took it seriously, but when he came to see me I understood that what we treated lightly was far more serious in Jim's mind. He came to tell me that Que had a girlfriend in Germany who was crazy about him. Her name was Kunda and Que was unfaithful to me. Jim assured me however, that if I were his wife, he would never be unfaithful. Jim was shy, and this kind of statement was as close to a proposition as he was capable of uttering.

Somehow I was neither shocked, nor upset. I don't think I was even surprised. Que was a very sexy guy and for him to be celibate for a year and a half was highly unlikely. He was in a very different world under very different circumstances which had nothing to do with us. I told Jim that a part of me was glad that someone offered him comfort and that I would not let this information spoil my reunion with Que. I was just so thrilled that the agony was drawing to a close that I would not allow it to be ruined. Maybe I was naïve, maybe stoic. Maybe I wasn't being completely honest with myself, but that was the position I took. Although I was flattered by Jim's attention, I had waited too long for Que's return and wasn't going to let anything influence my feelings for him. I kept assuring myself that he loved me and everything would be wonderful once he returned.

Christmas week drew to a close and early New Year's Eve found me in my grandmother's kitchen, in my slip, standing at the ironing board freshening up my little black dress. Que's brothers were picking me up to go out to celebrate his imminent homecoming. I was in some kind of reverie imagining our reunion when there was a banging on the door. We did not have a phone in our apartment but our neighbor did. She was banging on the door and screaming to me, "HE'S ON THE PHONE! HE'S ON THE PHONE!" Without any thought to my state of undress, I ran through the hall and up the stairs, laughing and crying and finally after a long year and a half, I heard his voice.

He told me that he had waited almost an hour to get his turn at the phone and that there was a long line of guys urging him to get off. All he could tell me was that he would be at Grand Central Station at 2 o'clock, to meet him there and that he loved me. I could hear the shouting in the background yelling for him to get off the phone. That was okay. He was in Fort Dix, New Jersey, he was safe, and he still loved me.

There was no sleep for me that night. I kept replaying that phone conversation over and over in my mind.

"Darling is that really you?" I had shouted, laughing and crying at the same time.

"It is! It is!" I think he was crying too. "Listen sweetheart," he shouted, "I've waited for nearly an hour for my turn at the phone and there's a whole bunch of guys yelling for me to get off. They are just as anxious as I was to make that call home."

I could hear them shouting and whistling in the background as he said, "I'm at Fort Dix, New Jersey and I'm scheduled to arrive and Grand Central Station on January 2nd at 2 in the afternoon. Will you be there?"

"Yes, yes of course! I'll be wearing my blue suit, the same one I wore when I came to meet you in Kansas. You'll recognize me by the blue of the suit and the huge grin on my face."

"I love you!" he shouted as I shouted the same words to him.

When I hung up, I sat in the chair in my neighbor's kitchen and the suppressed tears just poured out. In that rare moment, my grandmother allowed herself to abandon her practiced stoicism and expressed some weakness. She put her arms around me and together we wept.

New Year's Day was a day of preparation. I gave myself a manicure and pedicure. I fussed with my hair, deciding how to wear it. I took my suit out of the closet where it had hung patiently waiting for this day. I took out my best lingerie, my saved pair of silk stockings and my beautiful black suede ankle strap high heeled platform shoes, all saved for Que's homecoming. I laid everything out on the bed and hugged myself with joy. I was nervous, thrilled.

When I got to Grand Central Station, the scene was overwhelming. I had not given any thought to the fact that thousands of soldiers would be coming home. I just thought about mine, but when I found myself surrounded by the chaos of waiting wives, children, families, and soldiers, I began to panic. Trains kept arriving, one after the other, discharging hundreds of cheering soldiers, all looking strangely alike in their uniforms and with their backpacks. I started to run away, gasping for breath, my heart pounding out of my chest. I was overcome by weakness, my legs feeling like rubber. I leaned against a wall for support and I saw him running toward me. He found me! We could not let go of each other, kidding, laughing, crying, and kissing more. At last, we were together again.

I kept looking at him while we were on the train on our way home. There was something different in his eyes and he looked older. When he was not speaking or laughing, he had a hard set to his mouth. It came to me later on that he had gone into the army relatively carefree, a gentle boy-man of twenty-one, and came back a hardened man, no longer a boy at twenty-four. When he was drafted I was only nineteen, a fun loving young girl, but when he came back I was nervous and frightened with a problem we had never heard of in those days. Post-Traumatic Stress Disorder, or PTSD, was a popular disorder many soldiers had been diagnosed with after war, which included panic attacks and agoraphobia. We were still in love but we both had changed. The war had exacted its toll.

My Life Starts with Que

It had always been a curiosity: what could the name Que stand for? Quentin? Quigley? Quayle? None of the above. My Que's name has an entirely different history. From where did that name derive its uniqueness?

In the 1940s, teenagers socialized by hanging around on the streets. Malls had not yet been designed, there was no television, and the term video as in video games had not been coined. There was really not much more to do, especially if one had no money, as was generally the case.

I had the good fortune to have a steady job as a telegraph operator working for Western Union covering, in two week stints, people on vacation, which took me all over the city.

It was really great fun inasmuch as the offices to which I was sent were usually in hotels and I met people from all over the world. I realize that this was the world before internet, international phone service, and certainly Skype. Western Union was the line of communication at that time. At any rate, one night when I came down the steps of the elevated train I ran into a fellow who I knew casually. He introduced me to his three buddies, Red, Joey, and Que. We chatted for a bit and then I told them that I had to go home. Que offered to walk with me, which gave him the opportunity to ask me for a date the forthcoming Saturday night.

He was tall enough. I was five foot six, tall for my generation and he was five foot ten. He was very good looking, well built, polite and yet warm, he lived in the neighborhood and he even had a car. His mother shopped in my grandmother's store on Sunday mornings because, even though there were stores closer to where he lived, ours was the best store. On Sunday mornings, Que would drive his mother to our store because we had the largest selection of cheeses in the area and the Bogen's were great cheese aficionados. I would sometimes grudgingly help out on busy Sunday mornings and he was aware of me. I must admit that

I did not want to be there and was not aware of anyone. It was Sunday morning and after being out late Saturday night I wanted to be sleeping in my bed, not behind the counter of the grocery store.

On the Thursday prior to our first date he called and cancelled. I was mortified. He gave me some excuse that he had to work. His uncle, for whom he worked had a large trucking company and had gotten a call to send trucks up to several camps to pick up hundreds of trunks for kids who had just finished their summer vacations. Que said he couldn't refuse his uncle and I was not sure whether or not I believed him. I was piqued and answered him with a cold, "Fine, see you around."

The phone had barely reached its cradle when his friend Red came to the rescue.

"I know Que is working over the weekend and there's a good movie at the Loew's Pitkin," he said. "How about coming with me?"

Although I was really disappointed because I was attracted to Que, Red seemed affable enough and I really didn't know either one of them. The date was pleasant, we went out a few times and I did not hear from Que,

The Jewish Holidays came a few weeks later. We were members of the same Synagogue and I spotted Que sitting with his father, I was sitting on the extreme opposite side with my grandmother. He really looked so handsome in his dress-up clothes that I decided to abandon my pique and follow him if he walked out, pretending that it was accidental. He didn't walk out and I had enough of sitting there and so I walked out. Little did I know that he had the same plan, and there he was, right behind me. We took a long walk and when we got to the building in which I lived he walked me into the lobby. For the tenth time he begged me to forgive him. He had not called me because he thought I was interested in Red.

"Red is only a casual date and he and I both know that," I assured him. "And by the way, do you know how to dance?" He put his arm around me, started to sing, "I'm in the Mood for Love," a very popular song at that time and we danced our first dance in the lobby of the apartment house in which I lived.

The casual dating slowed down for me and after three months we were engaged. Of course the question of the name came up on that first momentous walk. It was then that I learned that he was the ninth of ten siblings, seven girls and three boys. Eight were married and most had children, enlarging the clan. Both parents were of large families and there were literally cousins by the dozens. When Seymour Bogen was eight years old, he bragged to his friends that his family was so large that there was a cousin for every letter of the alphabet. He was challenged on the letter "Q."

He thought for barely a moment and then he bravely said, "That's me. I'm Que." The name stuck and it really personified who he was; a really rugged individual in every sense. Although he remained Seymour to his family, to me, our children, my family and our friends, he was the one and only guy named Que; a special man with a special name. It appears so on his tombstone.

When the boys came home from the war, they were no longer boys. They were men. There was much to get accustomed to, but the big issue was to have our own home. We were desperate. We were married almost five years, I was pregnant and we were living with my grandparents in Brooklyn, sleeping in the old tiny room I had shared with my sister. We slept in a three-quarter bed, a cross between a single and a double bed. The room could barely accommodate even this diminutive bed, but apartments were scarce. Many returning servicemen and families were being housed in Quonset Huts in the Rockaways and the housing situation was one major mess so we had to appreciate that at least we had the privacy of our own room.

It was 1946 and the war was over. The boys were back from overseas and everyone was trying, or pretending to try to get back to some semblance of normal life. It sounds easier than it was. Average young men, hardly men, barely out of their teens, most of them nonviolent, particularly if they were Jewish, were drafted, sent to army camps, taught how to fight, given guns and told to go out and kill or be killed yourself, and they did what they had to. They go away sweet young twenty-year-old boys, come back hardened war weary men. I know mine did.

Que's brother suggested that we join him, his wife, and another couple, cousins of theirs at a bungalow colony in Arverne, Rockaway. We took them up on it. We were all childless and a good match. The men worked all week, but unlike the bungalow colonies in the mountains they were able to commute. Looking back at the jumble of life in all of the ensuing years it almost got lost in my memory but I am so glad to remember this. It was really a rare carefree period of life, freedom to loll on the beach all day, plenty of time to read mindless books or magazines, contemplate the miracle of the continuity of the ocean, the beautiful white sands and the enormity of the sky. Also it was a time to try to erase the inner turmoil of the war years, to challenge the demons of agoraphobia, to live with nature heretofore unknown: a time to reacquaint and to heal.

Ethel, a female cousin, was childless but pregnant for the fourth time. I was so glad that I did not want to be pregnant. Watching her agonize when she miscarried again was a sure turnoff for me. I really was afraid to have a baby and I knew it was time, but no thanks. I was almost twenty-four years old, married four years and terrified that if I had a baby, my fate would be similar to my mothers', dead at twenty-nine. She probably never should have had a second child. She left this earth when I was only one year old. Nobody was ever able to tell me what exactly she died from but those were very different years. It was not that uncommon for young women to die, during or after childbirth.

Well, I didn't want any part of it, or so I thought. Then, that winter it appeared that an accident may have occurred. I was beside myself. I cried a lot but that didn't help anything. When it turned out that I was only late, not pregnant, I started to cry. It dawned on me that I had a very normal instinct to have a child. My son was born in September of that year. I drove that poor doctor crazy every time I saw him. He assured me that he wouldn't let me die and he was right.

That Que and I loved each other was never in question, but the war had taken its toll on each of us. A trip to a hotel in the mountains seemed a good antidote for the awkwardness that we felt in my grandmother's home. The Laurels Country Club sounded like a good idea. I would have to take a week off from work–not a safe move at a time when defense work had ground to a halt and offices were downsizing in preparation for closing down. And so we went anyway and I lost my job.

Apparently our idea was not too original. The hotel was teeming with couples like ourselves, we even found people who we knew, but Que and I did find each other again. I do not suggest that our personal demons evaporated. Hardly so, but we were able to waltz around them, at that time and for years to come.

The trip home by bus was harrowing. It had snowed presenting a beautiful winter wonderland but the roads were iced over. There was a Rabbi sitting across the aisle from us and as we started descending the Wurtzboro Mountain, probably the highest in that range, the Rabbi started praying and I clung to Que and started crying. We crept down the mountain at a snail's pace, and I was sure, as the Rabbi continued praying that this was how it was all going to end. The bus would slide off the road, down the mountain and we would all be killed. I had gotten very good at creating horror scenarios and this was one of my best. Obviously it didn't happen and here I am sixty-six years later, remembering it clearly.

For the returning G.I.'s there were two paths from which to choose. There was college on the G.I. bill or join the work force. Most married men chose the latter, having already lost three or four years of their lives. Que also chose the latter. He and his brothers bought a small piece of rich Uncle Sam's trucking empire throwing us into debt; we had our first baby, a wonderful boy. I did not die in childbirth as I anticipated.

Then a miracle happened. One of Que's sisters, while visiting another sister in Far Rockaway, unexpectedly went into labor and had to be taken to St. Joseph's hospital to deliver the baby. Her roommate had a small apartment that had just been vacated and was available. We jumped on it. The apartment was originally an upper floor of a one family house. It consisted of three tiny rooms and a miniscule enclosed sleeping porch, a four room apartment if one stretched the imagination. The kitchen was antiquated. The stove was as old as I was, or perhaps older, standing on four legs, as was the ancient sink. The refrigerator was of indeterminable age. There was a kitchen dresser for pots, dishes, and all other necessities of a kitchen. There was room for a table and chairs, and a high chair and it was ours!

The largest room was about a twelve square feet and we decided that would be our bedroom. After our closet of a room at Grandma's, we needed some breathing room. The living room and baby room were each eight by ten and when I told the painter that I wanted one wall papered and painted the remaining walls in the living room he looked at me indignantly and said, "Do you think you are on Park Avenue?"

My answer to him was, "To me this is Park Avenue." I don't know whether or not he got it.

After five years, it was finally a home of our own, as it was. We were paying sixty-five dollars a month rent, which in 1947 was exorbitant. After a few months I determined that I would feverishly save every penny that I could and point my eyes in the direction of buying a house. The thermostat was in our apartment but the landlord had locked it at sixty-eight degrees. I got around that by putting a cold jar of baby food on the top of the thermostat which pushed the temperature down and sent the heat up. We managed for two winters there and when our son Bobby was two years old, we realized our dream. I found our first house.

It was built in 1895, the first one in Far Rockaway to have electricity, which was delivered to the second floor by way of wires running along the wall up the stairs to the four bedrooms and the bathroom. The kitchen was ancient but the house was charming. There were back to back fireplaces in the living room and dining room, pocket doors separating these rooms, window seats in the bedrooms, and a double window seat on the landing of the staircase. It was an old Dutch Colonial gem that needed a lot of work.

A man had this house built for his bride some fifty years before and they could no longer manage the steps. They wanted $9,500.00 for it and I offered $8,000.00. When the price was offered to the owner, he asked what kind of people we were. When he heard that it was an ex GI, his wife and baby, he agreed to my offer plus $400.00 for the broker. It was a deal and after the down payment we were pretty close to broke. However there is nothing better than a caring family and without even asking we were offered assistance in the form of a $1200.00 loan.

We got the electricity fixed, bought cheap kitchen cabinets and made the kitchen workable, bought a washing machine and had the place painted by the same painter, who turned out to be our next door neighbor. When I told him that I wanted the living room painted burgundy with sharp white trim and the same color under the chair rail in the dining room with wall paper above he gave me that same "Park Avenue" look, but did as I asked. The result was stunning which he had to reluctantly admit and we were beyond thrilled to find ourselves in our own home.

It took us about a year and a half to pay off our debt. We were poor but thrilled. We spent nothing on anything except absolute necessities and paying off that debt was the vehicle to freedom. We were free.

We meticulously paid back our business debt and then bought our first home by borrowing for the down payment. We became what I referred to as "house poor" but we were thrilled! A child, a home, a car, a business, and even a dog; this all added up to a normal life at last, after five years of marriage. I must admit that agoraphobia always lurked in the corner but I learned how to stay out of its way, most of the time.

The forthcoming years were rich with joys and sadness and one of the joys that evolved was my recognition of who my grandmother was. That happened because she allowed it. That aloof, non-touching, non-complimenting old woman had surrounded herself with an invisible wall to protect herself from any more of the unbearable pain she endured upon the loss of her oldest child, my mother, of which my sister and I were a constant reminder.

When my son Bobby was four, I had a daughter, Wendy, after two miscarriages. Bubby's health was beginning to catch up to her age and she started spending summers in my home. Zaida, her husband was a gentle sweet loving man but of minor consequence in the grocery store. That woman, that Bubby of mine ran the store, harbored two teenage orphans, was president of the Ladies' Auxiliary of her synagogue, and was the Sage of Blake Avenue. Everyone knew that if they had a problem, they could go to Mrs. Weinstein's apartment on a Sunday afternoon, and she would know what to do.

My Bubby, who I resented when I was growing up, who made me give her $5.00 out of my $18.00 paycheck and then spent all of it plus for a trousseau when I became engaged, who never let the l word – love – cross her lips, that woman fell in love with my children, her great grandchildren and forgot to keep her defenses up.

Her story unfurled and revealed itself to me during those summers, bit by bit and they are worth retelling.

Sometimes when you peel an onion it's a non-issue and at other times it can bring tears to your eyes. Looking back, life can be similar. Most conceptions, pregnancies, and births are nature's gifts and follow natural patterns, gestation follows insemination and childbirth of a hopefully normal child follows. For me that was hardly the case.

Our big plan was a large family; three or four children, but we all know about best laid plans. Bobby at two was a beautiful rambunctious child, big and bright, who sadly was asthmatic. I had some serious guilt about that; my father's asthma morphed into tuberculosis from which he died at forty-four. Although to this day I have tuberculosis scars in my lungs, the asthma skipped me and found a home in my baby. Nevertheless, it was time to have a second child after seven years of marriage. My pregnancy of four months was cause to celebrate when it happened. Our happiness crashed with a bloody mess sending me to the hospital for a procedure and a week's stay. I arrived at home empty handed and heartbroken on July 4th. That evening Que took Bobby and Shatzie, our adorable dog, down to the bay to see the fireworks. Shatzie panicked and ran away. This fed beautifully into my neurotic fear of loss: the baby, the dog, and I wondered what next? A neighbor passing by on a bus recognized Shatzie in someone's front yard and we went and rescued her. I got over my hysteria and once again started to follow my desire to enlarge our family. This time it only took three months for the same disaster to strike. Upon recovery it was time for action.

These were the doctor's orders: strengthen the sperm count. Que was to digest two packages of Jello, set or liquid, each day. No sex for three months. Also, after that period, early morning temperatures were to be recorded to establish time of ovulation. When the temp was ninety-six degrees, it was time for action right away and rest in bed for the next six hours.

Remarkably it worked. After a few attempts I was pregnant again. Now a new regimen began. Stilbesterol pills daily; five milligrams week one, ten milligrams week two on to 125 mg daily and then level off. No steps except when absolutely necessary. Our house was a colonial, filled with small flights of stairs. No lifting anything over ten pounds. Bobby was now three years old so it was not an issue. Avoid riding in cars. NO sex for the duration.

We followed the rules, and Wendy was born healthy and on time. Five days after coming home with her it happened, the bloodiest hemorrhage. The doctor actually came to the house, told me to get my butt down to the hospital or they would carry me out in a box. This was followed by a D&C, a week in the hospital away from my beautiful new baby and upon coming home I experienced fear and panic and realized that I would never go through this again. I would always be grateful that I had my two children and not run the risk of a similar trauma.

My intense hunger for a lovely home was now appeased.

At Bubby's we did not have a living room—we had a big dining room, table and chairs for family gatherings and Shabbat meals were much more important than a sofa and an easy chair or two. My sister and I never felt comfortable inviting anyone to come and sit around a dining room table, but now in my new home I had it all.

My furniture from the apartment came to life and sort of grew in stature in its new environment. The grey velvet couch looked beautiful and proud in the wonderful space allotted to it as did the two barrel shaped patterned club chairs. In my eyes, the round mahogany leather topped table, all the rage at that time, looked majestic topped by its tall lamp, standing there waiting to be admired. A house-warming gift from Bubby and Zaida was a console radio, and how grand it looked. Not a little table radio, but a console with a victrola, what a gift. Fill-ins would come gradually and hand me downs were gratefully accepted for the enclosed front porch and the extra bedrooms. We painted, polished and gussied them up and were very proud of our home. Yes, we had arrived!

I was the first one in my family to move out of Brooklyn and so my home became the family's Sunday destination.

Our corner house boasted a large back yard with the requisite swing set, another family gift. There was a great staircase with a banister for kids to chase around and we even had a ten-inch black and white television set with an enlarger in our front porch.

I had become very creative in the kitchen, and to this day could stretch a meal to accommodate any extras who were always welcome. Although my dining room table, which was really a dinette table, was hopelessly small, we managed and change would come later.

What a reversal of roles this was. I was no longer the misunderstood lonely unhappy child who acted out to get attention. I was no longer the rebellious young wife giving my grandmother grief living alone near my husband's army camp in some Godforsaken small town. We were an established family, owned our own home, with a mortgage, of course, and I had earned the respect of my family. I was no longer the "schleter," the bad one. I even had a road named for me, in the eyes of my family.

Two of my darling uncles, who were regular visitors, would call each other on Sunday morning and the conversation would go something like this: "Hello Morris, good morning. Are you going to Rockaway today?" "Sure, Norman, you too?" "Yes of course, so which way are you going? Are you taking the bridge or are you going by Esther Blvd?"

In those years before the building of Idlewild Airport, later to become JFK, before Rockaway Turnpike, the main artery from Brooklyn to Far Rockaway was Rockaway Boulevard. It was a pretty beat up old endless road which seemed to take forever, but the bridge had a toll and Rockaway Blvd. was free. Old habits die hard and even though the financial circumstances of these hard working immigrant business people, grocery store owners had improved considerably, that little gremlin watching the pennies was hard to eradicate. Invariably the conversation would end like this, "What the heck, I think I'll take the bridge today. What about you?" "Yeah, me too. I'll call Abe and tell him."

Bayswater and Bogen Years

How fortunate a child is to grow up in a family with a mother and father, being guided, validated, praised, and encouraged. Having experienced none of that, I recognize in retrospect the enormous need that drove me to prove to myself that I had value. Not only did I have to be a good wife, a good mother, a good homemaker, a good cook, a good baker, a good hostess – good, good, good – I had to sew drapes, make bedspreads, sit on the board and raise money for Hadassah, the board of the Sisterhood, the Board of the Civic Association, and I had to be President of the Parent Association at the same time. Yes Esther Bogen, you could do it all. You were even asked to run for public office but that was too far to push. Commute to Albany? Que would surely divorce me and anyway, Little Miss Agoraphobia would not let me leave my comfortable environs. It was time to slow down and exhale. Two hats at the same time were enough and they were Hadassah and President of the Parents Association of my children's elementary school. It was a lovely school indeed, nestled in the center of a lovely community.

While I was president of PS 104, we had a major election and a new Mayor was elected – John Lindsey. What a handsome, glamorous, rich man he was, but during his term of office, the beautiful Rockaways, part of Queens, was ultimately destroyed.

The trestle over Jamaica Bay and the link of the Long Island Railroad connecting Brooklyn to the Rockaways were converted to the subway system with a five cent fare. This move changed the demographics radically. No longer were the summer bungalows "vacation heaven" for thousands of renters. These bungalows along a five mile strip of beautiful pristine white sand beach became a haven for squatters and drunks. The city's most beautiful natural resource was mutilated. To add to the pity, a group of low rent housing projects was built, one of the seemingly necessary evils of that era.

Welfare was all the rage. "Teenagers! Have a baby and the city will take care of you with an apartment and money to live off." Not only was the area decimated but the schools were compromised as well and ultimately destroyed.

PS 104 in Bayswater, a small school with 600 students, was referred to as the Silk Stocking school. The principal, Mr. Grosfeld, knew every student by name, but change darkened the door. In its infinite wisdom the city imposed integration throughout the city and for our school it gerrymandered the borders to include two buildings of a project – sixty children, kindergarten to first grade to start with, with all of their younger siblings to follow, and there were many in the ensuing years. This threw the school into double session, but the whole concept was an ugly joke. The children, the "other" children, came by bus, and went home by bus. Integrate? Not at all. This small school was very local. The kids all lived within walking distance. These new students were poor children thrown into a milieu of the upper middle class and they knew that they didn't belong. It was all predictable. All of my pleading with the District Superintendent and the Board of Education leaders at 110 Livingston St. fell on deaf ears.

What they did do was allocate money for a wing eventually doubling the size of the school. They also recognized that there was need for more help and the Teacher Aide program was instituted. Mr. Grosfeld prevailed upon me to take the job with an assistant and I was put in charge of the two lunch sessions. Ostensibly the assistant principal was supervising but the children were so wild and out of control that this gentle man could not deal with them. One day he had to be taken to a doctor for chest pains. And so it became my job to get the lion into the cage.

"How did I handle it? With great difficulty, a strong whistle and a very loud imperious voice!" This is how it played out:

Mrs. Bogen blows the whistle. No response. Kids are running around, throwing food, and pushing each other. Mrs. Bogen intercepts a few jostling kids, they are pretty small, and continues to blow the whistle while holding two of them. More and more whistle blowing until finally it penetrates and the chaos starts to calm down. Mrs. Bogen continues to blow the whistle until they get the message and are seated and quiet. Now the message is articulated as follows, "When Mrs. Bogen blows the whistle you are to sit down and SHUT UP. If anyone does not understand what shut up means, raise your hand. Good. Now remember that. As long as you see me standing here there is to be no talking." One minute and the noise starts. I blow the whistle, "Who is talking while Mrs. Bogen is standing up here?" A few of them point to different kids, and I invite one of them to come up to the front and sit with me. Not a very happy experience and finally they are dismissed into the school yard of the gym and once again chaos reigns.

No matter how diligently we tried, not one mother of any of these kids would participate in the parent association or even come to a meeting. The school deteriorated and so did the entire neighborhood.

About thirty years later a young man came into my office with his son. He looked at me and said, "Aren't you Mrs. Bogen? I remember you from the lunch room."

"Aren't you Danny Schneider? I remember you from Mr. Grosfeld's office," I answered him. "Your teacher sent you there every day because you refused to have your almost chin length hair cut and she didn't like it."

The lovely moment ended with a warm smile and an affectionate hug.

It occurred to me recently that if I had been born a dog, I would have been an Alpha. This epiphany came while watching my daughter Wendy's dog Bijou at play with her best friend Luna. At eighteen months Bijou weighed about eighty pounds. She is a gorgeous Tibetan Mastiff. Luna is about a fourth of her size, a rather homely kind of mutt, generally sweet of temperament but hardly a show stopper a la *Petite Bijou*. However regardless of size and stature, there is no question about who is the Alpha and who is the Beta; Luna is the leader.

Throughout my school years I never enjoyed the popularity that some girls had, but that was the "then" me. At this point, my social life soared. Everything happened in the bubble of my Hadassah affiliation and my Alpha personality surfaced. My home became a focal point of gatherings of friends and my ideas were frequently applauded and embraced. I reveled in my popularity and caressed it gently. I didn't question it nor did I care. It just felt so good, so reassuring, so validating. When one of our friends, Hank, told me that I was a tropism, I didn't know if it was an insult or a compliment.

"Look it up," he said to me.

I ran to one of my best friends, the dictionary, and this is what it said: "An automatic movement in response to stimulation"

Afterwards he said to me, "Watch the way plants turn toward the sun and follow the sun, then you'll understand what I said."

One of the joys of having a place of our own was a telephone – something very much taken for granted by anyone born in the 1930's or later. But for those of us a decade older a phone in one's home was a beacon of luxury. There was usually a candy store, another lost dinosaur, on nearly every street and the telephone booth was the connecting link to the outside world, not only for sending but for receiving calls as well. There would always be some kids hanging around who would greedily vie for the chance to run and get someone to answer a call that was patiently waiting and to receive a penny or tip for their service. A penny could buy a cigarette, sometimes three for two cents accompanied by one wooden match per. In those years Ecstasy was not a pill, it was a penny cigarette.

My situation was one step up. We had a phone in the grocery store which sat diagonally across the street from where we lived. If there wasn't anyone there who could come and get me, at least a call back number could be held for me. The phone was in the back of the store, in a kitchen where we ate all of our meals except for Shabbat, making this almost the same as one's own phone and when a boy would ask me how to get in touch I would glibly say, "Let me give you my phone number!" My phone number, well it was half true because the back of the store was in fact our half home.

We also had an ace in the hole named Mrs. Koenig. This woman, who lived above us, owned the building which housed our apartment. She had great respect and affection for Bubby, my grandmother and she had her own phone. We were warned by Bubby that Mrs. Koenig's phone was strictly for an emergency and it was on that very phone, on New Year's Eve 1945 that Mrs. Koenig heard Que's voice for the first time in almost eighteen months. She came running down the steps crying and shouting, "Esther! Esther! Come quick! Your husband is on the phone!"

Armed with this knowledge it should not be too difficult to understand how glorious it was to live in one's own home with not one but two phones. These very instruments helped shape the path on which my life was to embark and which helped me to develop into the woman that I became.

One afternoon a young woman rang the backdoor bell. She lived on my street and told me that Hadassah, a Jewish organization was trying to start a group for young married women. I had no clue about what Hadassah was but I was hungry for the company of women like myself. It's not that I was lonely, I did have the friendship and company of my sister-in-law and her friends, but they were all much older than I and in a different time in life than mine. I greedily accepted the invitation to go to a meeting at the home of one of the officers of the Chapter and was intrigued by the energy in the room. As I said I had no idea what Hadassah stood for and so I raised my hand and asked.

"It is the women's Zionist organization of America and we would like you to take a position on the board," they replied.

How about that? I said to myself. *They don't even know me and they are giving me a position on the board.* Having never joined an organization before or been in the armed service I was ignorant to the fact that if you ever raise your hand you are considered a volunteer.

My lifetime association with Hadassah had begun. They

made me the sponsor captain. And what did that job entail? It was my responsibility to create a pyramid of phone callers who would each call a given number of members before each and every meeting to make sure they remembered to try to come to the meeting. Of course I had to instigate the phone calling.

And so my third child was born, but a child of a different nature and looking back over all of those years of involvement I continue to be grateful for the most wonderful friendships that developed over those years. I traveled through the whole gamut of positions from the naïve sponsor chairman, thru every vice presidency and of course through several terms as president. Even when money was tight we found ways to manage to take care of our commitment to the children who were rescued after the war and to the hospital our Hadassah women built. Whatever money I committed paid off tenfold in satisfaction and growth of character. Since this is a story about me, not about Hadassah I will leave it here at the present time, but only for the present.

Brooklyn of my youth was a world apart from Far Rockaway where my children grew up. We were never in conflict about who we were ethnically. We lived in a Jewish working class neighborhood: everybody was Jewish. There were some black people here and there but they kept to themselves and the few Irish boys who sometimes ran through the area, beating up the Jewish boys lived someplace else, I never knew where. We were not subjected to the constant cacophony of Christmas songs, we did not see Christmas trees for sale lined up in empty lots or on the streets, for sale, there was no Santa Claus on any street corner ringing a bell, nor did we know what a Christmas carol was. If there were churches, and as an adult I know that there were for Brooklyn was known as the borough of churches, there weren't any in the vicinity of Blake and Hindsdale, East New York, Brooklyn. Church bells were an unheard of sound and we did not know what Christmas cards looked like. Life was singular and isolated. Holidays were solemn and respected. Being the Weinstein orphan grandchildren was something of a position of status inasmuch as the Weinsteins owned the big grocery store on the corner and Bubby saw to it that we had new clothes for all major holidays.

Chanukah was not a major holiday, but it was one that was observed. Every one of the eight nights Zaida would light the appropriate candle, my sister and I would stand by and watch as he said the prayers, in Yiddish of course, and then he would give us each a penny or two. "Chanukah gelt" he would say and give each of us a kiss. That was it.

Most people tend to migrate towards people like themselves and making the move from the ghetto-like existence to the suburbs, which were quite mixed ethnically, we frequently found ourselves in the minority. This created an interesting dynamic. Instead of the drive to assimilate, which our predecessors had, my generation tended to seek out social and economic compatibility with people like themselves. We joined synagogues and Jewish organizations and began to observe the holidays which we previously tended to suffer at the behest of our parents or grandparents. This brings me to my story about Chanukah.

Having married into a family of ten siblings, my children were two out of twenty-two first cousins, many of whom were close in age. Although we were among the first to move to Bayswater, most of the others followed, and since I had a very large house, ours was most frequently the meeting place particularly for the lower half of the family. One Chanukah in the early 1950s I had a brainstorm. I decided to have a party for the children, all of them, and each aunt was to bring a small gift for each of the children. We would only spend around a dollar per child, but in those days, when $45-50 a week could support a family, one could get some kind of goodie for a child for a dollar. Each child had a big paper bag for his or her ten gifts and it was always a huge success. The following year we decided to make Chanukah even more prominent and gave children a small gift every night when we lit the candles, had our yearly Chanukah party with the family, and gave the best gift on the last night. Chanukah was a contender, Chanukah had achieved status.

Bobby's best friend was Jimmy Geraldi. The Geraldi's lived across the street in a big house. The whole family from grandparents down lived on different floors in the same house. For the Geraldi's, Christmas was a major thing. They decorated a big tree in the front garden, they decorated their grape arbor on the side of the house, and they went to midnight mass and then partied all night after church. They had the ritual of serving seven kinds of fish and seafood, and we were always invited. It was very festive and exciting, albeit a bit strange for us at the beginning. However we did get used to it and looked forward to going to the Geraldi's in the middle of the night on Christmas Eve. It was certainly huge!

Most people did not think of the religious ramifications of Christmas. It was a holiday to exchange gifts, to eat drink and be merry, as in that well known greeting "Merry Christmas."

After the holidays, one day I was driving the boys to school. They were in the first or second grade, six or seven years old. They were sitting in the back of the car and I could hear Jimmy saying to Bobby, "It's not fair. Chanukah is better than Christmas. You get a present for eight nights and I only get it on Christmas."

I chuckled quietly to myself and felt a sense of pride that somehow in a very small way we had helped Chanukah achieve status. It was no longer only a minor celebratory holiday; it became a holiday to be recognized with a story of which we could be proud. The custom we had started in our house in Far Rockaway was like a pebble in a pond, spreading out among all of our friends and theirs and so on and was actually germinated out of my Zaida's custom of giving my sister and me a penny or two each night when he lit the Chanukah candles.

These memoirs will be the only proof that I was alive and was witness to the events as I describe them. Their factuality cannot be proved or disproved inasmuch as they are solely products of my remembrance. However, I report them with complete honesty and clarity and with no attempt to rewrite history or reinvent myself.

In December of 1962 I turned forty. Having worried myself into a state of anxiety about completing my twenty-ninth year without dying as my mother had, my next emotional mountain to climb was getting past my fortieth birthday. I really should have been focusing on forty-fourth because that was when my father drew his last breath, literally, but somehow forty was the barrier to overcome in my mind's eye. My great capacity for worrying had developed into what could almost be rated as a talent, and I was busy anticipating my very likely imaginary demise.

I could visualize the entire scenario: my children would be devastated, my husband would fall into a zombie-like state of shock and the funeral would be enormous – probably as large as my son's Bar Mitzvah. Friends would gather in small groups, crying and hugging each other, my extended family would be dry-eyed and forlorn, stoic and suffering inwardly, as was their wont. Our Cantor would speak in glowing terms as would representatives of organizations, friends or family. It would certainly be a funeral one would be very proud of but I really didn't want any part of it. That was not the arena in which I wanted my star to shine.

As it turned out we had been invited to a dinner party at my friends Laura and Sy Mallis's home on the night before my fortieth birthday. They promised it was just going to be a quiet evening. It was a quiet evening with about forty immediate best friends. It was not at all uncommon for our parties to extend into the wee small hours of the mornings and as the party was in full swing, Que stepped up on a table, ripped off his shirt and exposed his white t-shirt on which he had painted, in large black letters *ESTHER IS 40!* The joke was on me.

I decided then and there to stop fixating on birthdays as harbingers of the end, but rather to greet each birthday as the gift that it is and to wear each and every one as a jeweled crown. I must admit that now as I approach my 90th birthday in a few weeks, that crown becomes heavier each year as I attach an additional jewel but I will gladly put up with the inconvenience.

Alas, when it happens, the funeral will not be nearly as grand as that imaginary one since most of the would-be attendees have already had theirs, and of my generation I am one of the sparse few left.

It is impossible to write about everything and this is not a chronology of my life. These are memoirs and I rely on triggers to suggest to me what to write about. One such trigger happened this past Saturday night.

The Bayswater Jewish Center has an active amateur thespian group who present a play each year to raise funds for the center. At the request of one of my nieces we went to my old neighborhood to see a play called "Brooklyn Boy," which ironically was about my old neighborhood. As we entered the building my niece remarked that the center had just celebrated its Fiftieth anniversary in that venue having previously been housed in an old large house and using a tent for Rosh Hashanah and Yom Kippur. I told her that Bobby's Bar Mitzvah, on September 17, 1960 was the first one held in what was then the new building and as we sat and waited for the play to begin, I reminisced about that long ago event.

That we ever got to that great event was a miracle in itself. It was unheard of in our family that a boy would not be bar mitzvah'd and getting Bobby to go to Hebrew school was a Herculean task. As we got into the "six months until" period it was time to be proactive and I engaged an ally, a private tutor. At this point Bobby realized there was no escape and got down to business. The date was September 17, 1960 for Synagogue and Kiddush and then a major Kiddush at home. A reception at the Colony Beach Club for 200 some odd people was scheduled for the following evening, Sunday the 18th at 5 o'clock. Everything was in order. The only thing over which I had no control was the weather, which was a bit nerve wracking since the at home event was hopefully to be out of doors. Well, you know what can happen to the best laid plans of mice and men. My nemesis was that infamous Hurricane Donna. We woke up Monday morning, the 12th, to darkening skies and the news that there would be no school that day. The kids were euphoric and I had a foreboding feeling of imminent serious trouble. The wind howled, the skies opened up and the streets began to flood.

Bayswater, where we lived is a peninsula jutting into Jamaica Bay and caressed by the ocean on the far side. The ocean raged and the bay, which was only one street away, became swollen and overflowed right down our street. In our kitchen we had a door that accessed the basement. One walked down four steps to a landing which had a door to the outside and then the rest of the steps down. I stood at the head of the stairs and as the water level outside continued to rise it started seeping in under the door. Fortunately I had the presence of mind to run downstairs and pull the freezer plug out of the wall. I had cooked and baked for weeks for the forthcoming Kiddush at home and it was all in the huge freezer chest. As the water in the basement rose, which it did, rapidly, the freezer turned on its side as if to float. I realized that we could be in danger, and decided we should get out while we could. Bobby hoisted Wendy, then eight years old, on his shoulders and I carried out the dog, Shatzie, in hip deep water a few blocks to a relative whose house was on higher ground.

Hurricane Donna was one of the worst of its kind to ever hit New York and Long Island certainly caught the brunt of it. Late in the day it was over. The house was spared but the basement was a disaster. Everything was afloat; boxes of things rolled up carpets, and of course my freezer. Our friend Hank had a sump pump and he got to the house before I got back. He and Que worked most of the night bailing in conjunction with the pump doing its job. By the next day, the water was gone and I nervously peeked into the freezer. It was perfect. No water had gotten in and everything was still frozen solid.

We plugged it back in and that angst was assuaged. The smell began and we started throwing things out. It smelled as if a mouse or a family of mice had died in the walls. How could I have people over in just four days with such a smell? So windows all over the place were opened, additional exhaust fans were borrowed and by Friday, September 16, 1960, normalcy was restored to the Bogen household.

Saturday, the big day, dawned beautifully. It was very mild and sunny and our at home event was going to be in the garden. As we walked into the synagogue we were thrilled. It was so beautiful, and Bobby was to be the first Bar Mitzvah boy in the new building of the Bayswater Jewish Center. If you are wondering whether or not he pulled it off, he did just great. He was certainly capable of doing it, he just resisted to give me grief, but when push came to shove, and with Mr. Friedman, sitting in the front row glaring at him, he smilingly came to the biemer, recited the blessings, read his haftorah perfectly and even made a lovely speech thanking his parents.

Everything at home went off beautifully, just as planned. At 4 o'clock the next day we were at the Colony Beach Club for pictures, my two men in tuxedos and Wendy and I in white. The place was just stunning; a lovely outdoor terrace right on the beach for appetizers, a huge circular bar and the striking dining room with black walls, white tablecloths and red flowers. This was a first for our crowd … a beach club reception was not yet the norm and we and our guests were thrilled. The band was fabulous and when the leader, a tall, handsome black fellow jumped off the bandstand, trumpet blaring "When the Saints Come Marching In," everybody was on his or her feet stomping after him as he traversed the whole room. It was truly a night to remember.

At the very end of the evening, as we sat with the caterer paying the bill, one of our cousins who had lingered after the others had left, came over and said to me, "Now this is the hard part."

I smiled at her and said, "Min, this is the most wonderful money I ever spent. It is not only my son's celebration but my grandmother and my grandfather were both here to celebrate with us."

One of my very few possessions that survived my disastrous fire is the Bar Mitzvah album. How it survived, albeit a slight bit damaged, I do not know, but I keep it open on a table in my living room and once in a while glance at some of the pictures and remember a time long ago and people long gone.

A few months after Bobby's Bar Mitzvah we had a serious snowfall and traffic around our area was at a standstill. Of course it was paradise for the children and major mop-up time for me. At that junction of my life I had still not outgrown my obsession about my lovely home being picture perfect and when the doorbell rang revealing a young couple with two youngsters in tow on a sled asking to come in I said, "Come right in, but you'll have to take your boots off." I had no idea who they were, what they wanted, and why they did not come to the back door like everybody else always did. Our house was on a corner and so the back door was just as accessible as the front door.

Once admitted I asked, "Can I help you?"

Their answer astounded me, "We came to see the house. We heard it is for sale."

I silently wondered what act of fate had sent them to me. The house was not on the market except in the far reaches of my mind. I was realizing that the time was coming when we should move on, Que and I had toyed briefly with the idea but it was only a germ of an idea.

The neighborhood had changed due to a low rent housing project which was erected a short distance away forcing undesirables and squatters out of that area and into the fringes of our area. In that era of relative innocence back doors were always left open, garage doors were never locked and usually they were usually left open. Our garage was free standing and a distance from the house. Our cars always sat in the driveway and the garage just had lots of stuff in it. One day, rummaging around in the rear of the garage, I discovered that a studio couch that had been stored in the garage standing upright against the wall was in fact playing host to somebody.

That did not sit too well with me but we put a lock on the garage door and put the incident to rest and life went on. However, a few weeks later another incident occurred making the appearance of this young couple even more amazing.

Over the years that we lived in this lovely old house, my kitchen evolved into a dream kitchen because of Tony. Tony was a very talented jack of all trades in construction but had no licenses and so earned his living by driving one of our trucks. However, every Saturday for months he and Que took apart and improved every facet of that old kitchen and turned mine into a conversation piece among friends and neighbors … it was the envy of my friends and a source of great pride and joy for me.

One morning as the kids were having breakfast before school and I was at the sink in front of the window, I glanced out on the street and was shocked to see a man poised over a woman who was sprawled with legs spread over my two garbage cans at the curb. They were fornicating right there in broad morning daylight in front of my window. I called the police and had a serious talk with Que that night.

We were loath to sell this wonderful old house, our first, our large Dutch Colonial with its shockingly modern kitchen that I had coveted and now had. We had to think about it long and hard and then the front doorbell rang and the dye was cast.

The couple had come to the wrong house. Unbeknownst to me the house across the street from mine was silently on the market. This couple knew the neighborhood; they had relatives on the street. They walked in; they looked around and asked me how much I wanted for it. They were ready to deal. I had no idea, not a clue of what to ask and told them I would call after discussing it with my husband, which I did.

We decided to double what we had paid for it and although they quibbled a bit, naturally, they were in love with the house and I had a new job.

There was a big decision to be considered. Should we stay in Bayswater or move to the Five Towns? The latter would probably be a better financial investment, but Bayswater was where the family lived; a huge family of cousins, aunts and uncles, all of us connected socially as well as otherwise. In the end family trumped investment and we bought another lovely house deeper in Bayswater.

The decision to stay in Bayswater presented a real challenge for me. Que wanted no part of the search, which was pretty consistent with his rather usual chauvinistic general post war attitude. The deal was that I was to find an acceptable house and then he would look at it and either approve or look some more. Although as I present it these many years later it does not sit too well, in the years of which I speak there was nothing unusual about these clearly defined roles in most marriages. Fortunately our taste in the housing arena ran a similar path and so I was undaunted and went about my quest.

Most people would assess a house as an inanimate

object, but not so for me. I knew that when I found the right house, it would speak to me. The problem was the limit of availability in my price range and the normal desire for any change to be one for the better. My broker dragged me from the ridiculous to the sublime, but none of the houses they showed me suggested a sense of home. I started to get a little nervous inasmuch as we had a contract and although there is always some flexibility we were committed to move on. I wasn't desperate yet but panic was hovering just around the corner.

Open school night at Wendy's school found me sitting in her seat next to her classmate Marcy's mother. We had an acquaintance from other such events and so engaged in casual chit chat. In the course of conversation I mentioned my difficulty in finding a house and she mentioned that her next-door neighbor had their house on the market but seemed to have changed his mind. She was aware that some work was taking place, some new furniture being brought in and other indications that perhaps they had decided to stay. Nevertheless she told me his name and the street address. The next day I scoped out the street and the house.

The street was lovely with old huge trees on both sides of

the road which reached out to each other creating an arbor and ending in a cul-de-sac. There were six, large-sized, well-kept houses with front and rear gardens separated by broad driveways, leading to two-car garages on the other side of the street. All tallied, there were thirteen houses on the street, including a massive mansion on a vast garden standing at the entrée to the street. I liked the whole ambiance and decided I had nothing to lose by making an aggressive move.

I went home and dialed the number Marcy's mother had given me. When the owner answered the phone I said, "I understand you had been interested in selling your home and wonder if you are still considering it?"

"Who told you about my house?" he answered.

"It was you next door neighbor, Edna. My name is Esther Bogen and our daughters are in the same class."

His response astounded me. "Did you say Bogen? Is your husband in the trucking business? I do business with the Bogen boys."

Talk about serendipity! When I told him he was one and the same, he invited me to come over. Wasting no time, I promptly jumped into my car and ran over with my heart in my mouth. Would I like the house would he change his mind again and decide to sell and would the price fall into my range?

I swallowed hard, rang the doorbell and he opened the door. I walked in and the house said, *Welcome Esther. You can live here. You can love me and I can love you back. Don't let me go.* Oh my God. I found it and it wasn't even for sale, but maybe, just maybe, it could be. In the course of conversation the owner offered his reason for having put the house, which he and his wife loved, on the market. Their sixteen-year-old daughter had started Far Rockaway High School and ugliness followed her there. She was a bit chubby and the girls in her previous school had snubbed her and taunted her with the nickname "Fat Laurie," which now made her despondent. She was their youngest child and they were devastated to watch her torment and thought it would be best to move to another area where she could start over with different children. We agreed that it was fate that brought us together and that he should sell the house to me. I told him that I could not spend more than $25,000 and he agreed to meet my offer, although we both knew that it was worth more. There was only one sticking point. During their ambivalent period of indecision they decided to stay and had ordered new carpeting for the living and dining rooms, a very large space. If I was willing to split the cost, some $800, we had a deal. Yes, yes, we had a deal. All I had to do was come back that night with Que. I felt safe. I knew he would be just as receptive as I was and we were going to have a new house, no, a new home!

One of the joys of this house was its garden, although admittedly I did not appreciate it from the onset. It felt a bit claustrophobic at first because there were driveways on either side leading up to garages and our old house was on a corner and wide open. However I became adjusted to the privacy it offered and the quiet. Another thing I did not appreciate right away was the abundance of Tiger Lilies and purple Irises in the far corners of the back garden until I became aware of Van Gogh's famous paintings of Irises in Provence. I then looked at them with a different eye and learned to love them. There was also a lovely tree that blossomed beautifully in the spring and then gave birth to seven Bosc pears in the summer. My Bubby spent her summers with us and every morning she would go out and visit the pears, reporting back to me that they were all there and were not mysteriously attacked during the night by some beastly bird or squirrel.

As the years passed, of course, the young pear tree matured and bore more fruit in the natural order of things.

What is a house in the suburbs without a dog? So we got a parade of them. Accepting the first one was not too easy for me since I was always petrified of dogs. If I walked on a street and saw a dog coming in my direction, even on a leash, I would cross the street, but I was determined that my children would not have that unreasonable fear. When Bobby was an infant, a dog in our immediate area had a litter. A young boy came to my apartment carrying a tiny puppy and asked me if I could take it. I, the adult that I was, mother of a young boy, was afraid of that tiny puppy. But, I agreed to take it in and found a box for her to call home. We named the dog Shatzie and I learned to adore that dog. I would get down on the floor, look at her and say, "Shatzie, shaina madela," translated to "sweetheart, beautiful girl," and that dog would wag her tail and scoot around sideways with joy. Everybody loved Shatzie, that Cocker Spaniel mutt with the waggy sideways backside.

When she died, we decided to adopt a rescue dog. This one was beautiful: bigger than Shatzie but with the same coloring so the kids named her Shatzie II. Nobody warned us that this one was a terrible chewer. Shortly after she arrived, we went to the beach and left her in the open door garage on a long lead with food and plenty of water. There was a day bed in the garage and so we knew she would be comfortable. When we got home she was sitting on the day bed completely surrounded by all of the innards. It was an amazingly hysterical sight but we realized that we could not trust her and since she would have to be home alone most of the time, this was not a good match. We returned her to her owner understanding why the owner was anxious to give her away.

Very shortly after that another rescue dog arrived. My aunt and uncle were moving into a new apartment in a building that did not permit pets. They had a huge Black masked brindle German boxer named Major who was about five years old. We took him in. He was very handsome but he had two serious faults. When we would sit at the kitchen table at dinner, he would situate himself under the table and fart. This is one large breed and his expelling of gas was like a foul smelling explosion. The kids would get hysterical but I didn't appreciate it. However that was the least of the problems. He had an irrepressible hatred of cats and if he spotted one, there was no way to restrain him on the leash. He would demolish the cat and bring it home to me as a gift.

There was a male couple living across from us and they had several cats. Major would hang around the front door waiting for someone to come in or go out and he would dash across the street and find one and do his dirty work. He had to go. Bobby was devastated worrying that I would send him to the dog pound, but we found someone who knew someone who had a farm. And away he went. We were ready for the next dog when someone in our family who had a friend, a gentle gay gentleman who was moving to Florida was looking for a home for his black Lab, named Champ. Champ was a champ and we had him for years, watching his snout turn gray with age and his hind legs stiffen with arthritis.

When he became incontinent it was time to put him down and as I sat crying in the Vet's office he told us a story.

For three days a dog was hanging around the junior high school. When nobody claimed the dog the principal announced that he would have to call the ASPCA. Understanding what that meant, one boy took the dog home but they already had a dog. The parents knew of a woman in the neighborhood who rescued abandoned animals, they called her and she was paying the vet to house the dog and look for a new home for him. She could not keep him inasmuch as she was a polio victim and walked with the aid of leg braces and two canes, but she was cautious about whom she would allow to adopt the dog. We had to sign an agreement as to how much freedom the dog would have etc.

We passed muster and adopted Chester, but the name had to change. I was Esther long before he was Chester. He was a white medium sized mixed breed with large patches of brown on his torso and his snout. He looked like a small pinto pony and so we named him Pinto. That dog didn't have a voice for over a month. He would cower when he heard a plane, shaking with fear, but we showered him with affection and he remembered how to bark all right. He also learned how to smile. People were astonished as I would say to him, "Pinto, show me your teeth" and he would smile vigorously. At this point Que was no longer working and he and Pinto were buddies. When Que died two years later, I hired a dog walker to take care of his needs after school and in the evening.

Two years later I had remarried, and five years after that

it was time to sell the house and move to an apartment. The man who purchased my house was the Secretary to the permanent mission from Ghana at the U.N. He had five children and wanted a permanent home for them here in the States. On both occasions that he came in a chauffeured car to see the house he brought two children and while we talked business the kids busied themselves with Pinto. They loved him and he loved the attention he was getting from them. Although I loved Pinto and cried inwardly when I made the offer he was accepted as a gift with a great smile from Mr. Owasu and screams of delight from the children. Having a dog in an upstairs apartment where both people worked full time was fully trumped by his remaining in his home with his run in the backyard and children who already loved him. About a week after we moved I went back to see him. He greeted me as he did all visitors, no whining, no reproachful looks, no signs of disapproval, nothing. It was a relief. I knew I had done the right thing, and when I said to him "Pinto, get in the house," he just obediently went into the house and did not look back.

That was my last pet. I am an apartment dweller, a very appropriate way of life at my stage and although I sometimes think of how nice it would be to have a not too large well behaved cuddly dog or maybe even a cat when I think of a leash or a litter box I know it's not for me, not now anyway.

Bill Friedman was a young pediatrician when Bobby was born. He had just come back from his honeymoon with his new bride, a recently widowed rich young woman from Belle Harbor and had taken office space in Bayswater, later to move to the other side of town. He came to see Bobby the day of the Briss and fell in love with him. Since patients were sparse that first year, he would have me bring Bobby over once a week and we would chart his incredible growth, just for fun. There was no consideration of breast-feeding in that era. I was given salts to inhibit milk forming and my breasts were bound, in the hospital. By the time I went home, after almost a week in the hospital, I was as weak as a kitten and wasn't even present at the Briss. We did not call it breast-feeding. It was referred to as nursing and just was not done anymore at that time.

Bobby grew at an amazing pace, a cheerful, beautiful, dimpled, talkative little boy who refused to walk until he was eighteen months old and about thirty-five pounds. He was a handful, though, mischievous and teasing, but I adored him. I spoiled him. It was so easy for me to pour over him the love and affection I never experienced as a child. Maybe if we had guidelines for child rearing I would have held back somewhat, but I doubt it. Did I mention that I got my very first doll as a child for my eleventh birthday from my dear Aunt Sadie? Well now I had a real live doll, all my own and it was so gratifying. However, when he was thirteen months old, my bubble burst. I heard it for the first time; the wheeze of asthma. I knew that sound well. My father was an asthmatic who died of tuberculosis at a young age. I lived my early childhood surrounded by that dreadful sound and I had transferred that horrible future to my adorable son. I knew it was genetic because when my father was dying in the hospital, my sister Bea and I had to have frequent chest x-rays.

To say I was devastated would be a huge understatement. Through me, my child had inherited this awful disease. The only saving grace was that Dr. Bill advised me that the probability of his outgrowing it during puberty, since it had come so early in his life, was very much in his favor, and outgrow it he did. But it took a pretty strong toll on his early life and mine.

School was never his favorite pastime and his first grade teacher, Miss McKenna, only worsened the situation. She was a nasty old biddy of undetermined age, but old enough for my friend Stanley, who is twenty-five years older than Bobby, to have had her in his first grade also, with a less than kind remembrance. She didn't like children, particularly boys, and most assuredly boys who were big for their age. She did not understand that a big boy of six was no more mature than a small boy of six. One day, the kindergarten class was brought in to see what a first grade class looked like, and Bobby excitedly greeted one of his cousins. She made him stand in the corner with a wastebasket over his head. Not a very good foundation for a love of school.

We struggled through the school years. Although he had an above average IQ, his resistance and inappropriate sense of humor gave me much grief and we finally decided that private high school was the way to go. Vietnam happened in his senior year and he threatened to leave school and join the army.

This is what his father said to him, "Bob, I am a business

man. When I invest in something I expect to see a return. Public school is free, but I sent you to a private school at great expense and I expect to see a diploma. Although you are twenty-five years younger and four inches taller than I, if you ever threaten to quit school again, I will invite you into the backyard and flatten you. Do you understand?"

He understood all right, and gave his father the diploma upon graduation.

My mother was twenty-eight when I was born. She died shortly after her twenty-ninth birthday. I was twenty-nine when Wendy was born, after two miscarriages, an at-risk pregnancy and a near death hemorrhage when she was one week old. Surely death was around the corner for me. So it was prudent to worry, and worrying always has been and remains my special expertise. At that time the object of my angst was my thirtieth birthday, which I was afraid would signal the death knoll. Well obviously if I had known then that at eighty-eight, I would start writing about it, I could have saved a lot of wasted worrying for something better. Thirty came and went and I loved being a mom.

Wendy was a very different story. She was a beautiful, healthy, cheerful good little girl. She learned early on how to deal with her big brother's teasing. We had a film that just about spelled it out. Que was mowing the lawn and six year old Bobby was collecting the cuttings and pouring them over two year old Wendy's head. Instead of crying, which he expected her to do, she was laughing. That was her personality. She always was and remains a pragmatist.

Ballet school started at three years old. We began taking trips to Lincoln Center when Wendy was about five and we both remain great fans of the Ballet. School for Wendy was a breeze. She was smart, she was focused, she knew what was expected of her and she complied. It was the 1950s. But then the 1960s burst on the scene; the Beatles, Rock and Roll, marijuana, and Woodstock. Wendy was seventeen and had her own car - a Volkswagen Beetle.

Bobby was born in 1947, Wendy was born in 1951. That era was known as "the age of innocence." Television was still in its infancy. There were seven stations. News was reported four times a day. There was the morning news, news at noon, again at six o'clock and then again at eleven in the evening. One of the channels showed a movie after the late news; Million Dollar Movie, and they showed the same film every night for a week. They also showed it during the late afternoon.

I remember that Bobby watched "A Walk in the Sun" every day for a week, and his father watched it every night for a week. Then they would discuss the most intimate details to see who got it right. There were some lines that they both loved and they would throw them to each other and burst into laughter. There was no such thing as cable, with news in your face twenty-four hours a day. When you went to the movies, they had a newsreel, "Pathé News," and that seemed to be enough.

We knew that the perfect family was a mother, a father an older brother, a younger sister and then maybe a little one of whatever gender. Fathers went to work. Mothers stayed home and cleaned, cooked, baked, did laundry, and looked refreshed and nicely dressed when father came home. Then everyone sat around the dinner table and chatted amiably while mother presented the casserole of the evening. Maybe big brother gently teased little sister who would pout a bit and look down and smooth her pretty skirt over its crinoline. And of course, father always knew best!

If the 50s were an age of innocence, then the tumultuous 60s and 70s were a time of discovery, discontent, and rebellion.

We began to understand that the best instrument of control was instilling fear, big time fear like fear of Communism, fear of the Atom Bomb, and above all fear of the A bomb in the hands of communists out in the Soviet Union. That was the general climate in the U.S. but it was abstract. It was always there but not at your doorstep, that is until a strange word entered our vocabulary; Vietnam and accompanying it was those dreaded words "the draft." Again young men, my son included, had to register upon reaching eighteen years of age.

When Bobby was called up, his childhood battle with asthma was a gift of deferment, but the wake-up call was loud and clear. That Vietnam War was a horror and a disgrace. Young men were being slaughtered by the thousands, and the youth in this country, their parents, their classmates, their professors and their friends were protesting, sometimes violently. They burned the Chief of Staff Westmoreland's effigy in front of the Astor Hotel, in New York. They had sit-downs in colleges, demonstrations at the capitol, rallies, marches, and concerts; they did everything they could think of to make their protesting heard. "Hell no, we won't go!" was the rallying cry, and many went to Canada to avoid going.

The kids went wild and the country was changed forever. Recreational drugs became virtually the norm and my kids were swept up in the whole atmosphere of the era. Nearly everyone was smoking pot, my more avant-garde friends included. With my generation it was an occasional thing and although I did join them from time to time, I did not like the way it made me feel. I preferred my martini. Those were wild years; we partied, we drank, we smoked and we flirted, but we always worried a lot about our kids. Our erstwhile Governor Rockefeller, a married man who had a heart attack and died in the arms of his mistress had signed a law that sent kids to jail for possession of marijuana – grass, pot, weed –whatever you want to call it. We didn't have a war anymore, we possessed the most atom bombs, and the Soviet Union was on the decline. We needed an ogre, and an ogre it turned out to be, to this very day. We had the War on Drugs.

At this point Bobby was in his early twenties and engaged, and Wendy was attending Queens College before switching to Buffalo. They were great friends, and our house, which was always open to their friends, was frequently buzzing with young people. When they would confine themselves to Wendy's room, we knew they were smoking pot and we were not hypocritical about it. If alcohol was acceptable in reasonable amounts, who were we to say marijuana was not? What we did constantly caution them about was the fact that it was illegal and carried terrible consequences. The law was tough and blindly unfair. I have always felt and still do that pot should be legalized and controlled and sold only to adults in the same manner as alcohol or cigarettes. Realistically, prohibition spawned bootleggers and drug prohibition spawns drug dealers and illegal drug traffic. It didn't, and doesn't make sense.

Thankfully, my kids got through that stage of their lives without any misfortune, but it surely was a nerve wracking and worrisome experience.

The thirty-three years of my marriage to Que Bogen carved and framed my persona. The early years were, of course the most difficult. Money was tight and we were building a business. We were experiencing a serious period of re-adjustment to each other. Then there were children. We, as Jews, are very big on education, but in those years there were no guidelines for the most important job of one's life; child rearing. We all did the best that we could and let our instincts direct us, and are grateful for the good results.

Speaking of education, it took a long time for me to forgive myself for not having gone to college. Perhaps if Que had not died when we were both so young I would have followed my appetite to learn, formally. After I got over the initial shock of his death and adjusted to the fact that I was alone, it was time to make some decisions. I consulted a college counselor. In order to accomplish anything, I would have to attend classes for thirteen hours a week and do at least thirteen hours of homework, while working full time. I had just started to socialize and decided that being the social person that I am, college was not the right option for me.

By then I had gotten over the idea that had haunted me for the previous forty years. I was under the impression that anyone who had gone to college and had the advantage of education was smarter than I was. After all, they knew things of which I had no knowledge.

One night at a cocktail party my darling cousin Mickey put his arm around my shoulder and said to me, "Cousin, don't you know that 5% of the people are smarter than most of people, and you are right up there?" I was stunned! Mickey, the educated popular conversationalist guy that he was, thought that about me. It was time to reevaluate my thinking and pay a little more attention to those who I thought were automatically brainier than I. I did not have that degree and I discovered that although perhaps they were a bit more polished, many of the people with degrees were not deep thinkers. As a matter of fact I decided to let go of that misguided concept and just work at developing myself.

And so, during my "Bogen Years" as circumstances permitted, we started broadening our horizons. We expanded our cultural interests via theater, concerts, ballets, and museums. We traveled to exotic places in the late 60s and early 70s: Hawaii, Spain, Greece, and the Orient. When our friends were going to London and Rome, we were going to Tokyo and Hong Kong. When they went to Paris we went to the Greek Islands.

Que was a rugged individual. Being one of ten siblings and having been brought up in a huge mass of cousins, his yearning and dynamic was to be different. So different we were and growing all of the time. And then, he died.

It was just as abrupt as that. I was on my own, but he had done a good job. He had pushed me and prodded me. I fought back a lot because he was so controlling, but it was just that quality in him that forced me to grow. I am eternally grateful to him for that. He prepared me for the vicissitudes of life that would follow.

There are a wealth of stories that can be told about my years married to Que Bogen. I loved that it was such a large family and I was accepted as one of them. That was a big trick considering there were seven sisters. The other two sisters-in-law, who were married to Que's brothers, did not fare as well as I did, but I don't think it meant as much to them as it did to me. There was a wonderful sense of security that I experienced and I nurtured it. Of course there were obstacles from time to time, but it was my intention that my children would experience what I perceived to be the beautiful sense of family in a way that I did not as a small child. Obstacles were either overcome or overlooked and it was a great piece of life, all of those cousins living in Bayswater and all of those cousins growing up at the beach club, or all of the cousins from the lower half of the family celebrating holidays at our house. Although it was hard work I was happy and proud to do it. I wanted or needed to be validated and I was.

I cannot say that I was particularly fond of my mother-in-law. She was obese where the females in my family, my grandmother and my aunts, were all slim. Although she came to America as a girl of sixteen, she never learned to read or write, not too uncommon then because she went to work in a factory until she married and produced ten children, one every two years. I could not understand it. I was not accustomed to that. My grandmother who had had seven children read a newspaper every day and two of them on the weekend. She could read and recite her prayer book as well as any man, which was something of a phenomenon. She ran a busy grocery store which supported two families and could add up a column of figures scribbled with a small pencil which she moistened from time to time as fast as you could write them. She also had two preteen girls for whom she provided and guided until they married. Given all of that, although I showed respect to my mother-in-law, I admit that it was really only lip service. I never felt that having an active life in bed was a claim to fame.

She overtly favored her daughters and their children. Usually, in most Jewish families, the sons are the favored ones given the most opportunities for education. Not so in this family. In this family the boys worked in the summer on their Uncle's trucks from the time they were fourteen and when they reached sixteen it was understood that they would leave school and go to work to help support the parents and whoever else was at home. With Que, when his time came, it was to help his parents make a big wedding for his sister. Que's father was a small man with a big need to feel big; a big wedding, which he could not pay for, would make him feel big. He did. He had a Napoleon complex and lorded over his daughters, most of whom were married with children. When they came to his home they were not allowed to wear lipstick or nail polish, and they acquiesced, but I didn't. Instead I charmed him, but more than that he had delusions about me. After all, I was Mrs. Weinstein's granddaughter and the perception was that the Weinstein's must have money, having that big grocery store during such hard times.

As it turned out, Que got drafted and we did not get married until after his father died. I think that was fortuitous because after he died I came across some of Que's High School report cards at this mother's house. He was a very good student and deserved the opportunity to further his education with their encouragement. Instead they encouraged him to leave school and go to work. By the time he came home from the war it was too late. His brothers had already started the wheels turning on a business for the three of them and the path was established. In the end it turned out fine but I could never find it in my heart to understand and forgive their ignorance.

———————

My grandmother once told me that in life one should not look up, that's too easy. One should always look back and remember from whence you came. I never forgot that sagacious offering and am always in awe of where I am, in relationship to from where I came. Everyone who knows me has heard me comment, "Look at me, yenta from Blake Avenue," having to do with perhaps the smallest of things to the most wonderful of things. I never take anything for granted and always remember to see myself on a ladder and look down from whence I came. It has been a great adventure with a very short list of things yet left undone. They are these memoirs on which I am casually working and also a better understanding of the mysterious Kabbalah. Perhaps there are a few more hidden items but in my challenge box the Kabbalah stares at me. It tantalizes me, but not randomly, for there are specifics. I know that in the Kabbalah numbers have very powerful sequences, and in my personal experience they assuredly do.

When Que died of a brain aneurysm, he was only fifty-four years old. I was looking through the strongbox for his social security card and came across the cablegram he had sent me thirty years before in 1945. It was dated 12/25/45 and read, "Loading from LeHavre 12/26/45. See you soon. All my love, Que." He started his journey home 12/26/45, arrived in the States 12/31/45, and came home 1/2/46.

12/25/45, 12/26/45, 12/31/45, 1/2/46.

On a snowy day on 12/25/47 I had a small dinner party with Que's brothers and their wives. During the event Que developed a monstrous headache, something very alien to him, and could not remain at the party. As the evening evolved, his forehead began to swell and by the next, 12/26/47, day he looked like a man from Mars. The snowy day had become a blizzard, and a doctor fought his way around the corner from which we lived, gave him a shot of Penicillin, which was very new at that time, and told us we had to call a specialist. There I was with my three month old infant and this fearsome problem confronting me. Again I felt that this was it, the final irony after all of the angst these past four years, but not so. The specialist came, a small man with a heavy German accent, pince nez and high leather boots. He ordered hospitalization immediately. They attached Que to a machine to drain his sinuses for four days and on 12/31/47 they told me that he would be okay. He came home 1/2/48.

12/25/47, 12/26/47, 12/31/47, 1/2/48: Familiar numbers.

In 1975 we were scheduled to go to Israel on Christmas day with some friends and the Belle Harbor Jewish Center. Everything was paid for and in order. However on 12/25/75 following a severe headache for several days, we took him to St. Joseph's Hospital against his protests and insistence that we were going, he was diagnosed with a brain aneurysm. On December 26, we took him by ambulance to N.Y.U. Hospital, during which time he started his journey to death; he died December 31, and we buried him January 2, 1976.

12/25/75, 12/26/75. 12/31/75, 1/2/76.

Looking back and seeing that these were thirty years to the day that he returned from the army, a combat soldier, who survived in spite of the odds, who was in a foxhole when it took a hit and five guys died and he walked, who was in a jeep that exploded and three guys died and he walked, who came home relatively whole and survived thirty years exactly. These numbers must mean something but to me they are the mystery of life. I hope that before it is all over for me I will find the key, and perhaps exploring the Kabbalah a bit will provide that key.

Suddenly Single

We all go through various stages of metamorphosis, from infancy to childhood, from childhood to youth, and from youth to adulthood. We then push through the many challenges that confront us as adults and on into our senior years. There are some specifics that create radical changes; death of a parent, or death of a child or spouse. All of these losses are dreadful, but death of a spouse gives birth to many new decisions never before been confronted. One has only to sit in on a bereavement group session to learn how devastating this can be, questioning one's very being. What am I now? Am I half a person? Will I be able to maintain financial security? Will I always be alone? Will I always see myself as a bereaved widow? Will I ever feel normal again?

Can I, after thirty-three years of marriage ever become single again and face a new life with another person?

We have our choices, do we not? When opportunity knocks we have to have the interest to recognize it and the courage to accept it and move on.

Marriage is a comfortable shawl under which we wrap ourselves. It's a sense of belonging to common society, especially if one lives a suburban life and surely if one is middle age or older. Life's plan is to age graciously with one's spouse, one's life partner. But it doesn't always work out that way. Two become one, sometimes by death and sometimes by design. I don't think anyone really knows how he or she is going to react to being in an entirely different place in life than planned or anticipated; suddenly one where there used to be two.

What do you do? Where do you go? Who do you turn to? Why do you get angry when people tell you that you will adjust and go on, unless they have been there they don't get it. But the clock doesn't stop. The old cliché that time waits for no man is in fact true, and you do adjust, unless you are of the mind that without your partner you are only half a person. Maybe it's time to remember who you were before marriage, or maybe it's time to revisit yourself and perhaps do a little reinventing. Yes, that's it. Mourn while you have to and then let go. Close the door, turn the page; a new chapter has to begin and what happens in this new chapter is strictly your own choice.

The bereavement group hears one of the participants lamenting that if he had given the thief the wallet he probably would not have been shot and now he would not be half a person.

"Hold on," the therapist declares, "what were you before marriage? Let me hear from all of you."

Looking straight at me he asks me to tell him. I think for a moment and tell him that I was dynamite whereupon he assures me that not only was I dynamite but I still am and always will be. WOW! Is that possible? Am I still the interesting exciting person I was as a young woman? Do I have the courage to give up the mantle of grief and go out and meet the world as a widow? I detest that word. It conjures up black widow's clothes, visits to the cemetery and tears, depression, dependence on the kindness of others. I cannot wear that title. I have to be a single woman. Ms. Bogen - yes that's who I have to be - Ms. Bogen; single woman at fifty-three years of age. Life does hand out its challengers, doesn't it, and this was only the beginning.

His name was Danny, my first date as a recently single woman at age fifty-three. That name, Danny, always found a soft spot in my heart. It could have been because of the romantic Irish song "Danny Boy." I used to think so but I recently had an epiphany. One summer when I was about twelve years old a new boy suddenly appeared on our street. He was a little older, he was very handsome and he smoked cigarettes in the street. I was at a loss. I was too shy to even think of flirting with him or even talking with him, but I was star struck. The chatter about him was that he was a bad boy - stay away from him - he'd been away, which was a genteel term for reform school. That made him even more gorgeous and even more unattainable. As suddenly as he had appeared, that is how suddenly he disappeared. I never knew what happened to him and forgot that he ever existed until today. So, back to the Danny of my current story, the one with the romantic name.

He was a fix-up, an introduction. Here we both were, two adults suddenly cast to the vagaries of singlehood, in a world to which we were strangers. I was recently widowed and he was barely on the cusp of a divorce. He was involved in an on and off affair with a married woman for many years. When his wife caught wind of it he broke if off. After a period of reconciliation and promises it would start up again, same woman. Finally his wife bit the bullet and kicked him out. His paramour was delighted. She wanted to divorce her husband and marry him but he wanted no part of that. He wanted to explore the single world. Danny was another bad boy, and there was nobody around to warn me to stay away.

On that first date, he said something to me that you must agree was rather amusing. As we parted after a lovely dinner he told me that he would call me to go out again and then he said, "You are very nice; I really like you but please don't fall in love with me."

"Thank you," I said. "I'll be careful." When I got into my house, I evaluated the evening. Nice guy, attractive, educated, lawyer, good conversationalist and so on, but what was that comment all about? A few nights later a friend and I went to a Singles Rap Session, and who else was there but Danny. We were pleased to see each other and he asked me for a date. I was pleased to see him again and accepted whereupon again he said, "Just don't fall in love with me."

At this point I turned to him and said, "Danny, you have it all wrong. I'm not going to fall in love with you. You are going to fall in love with me."

He looked at me dumbfounded. And he did. For the next few months we learned a great deal about life outside of marriage, explored some unusual scenes that neither of us ever knew existed. But I never fell in love with him and he was quite distraught when I told him I was getting married.

I introduced him to a stunning woman who he married and divorced after fifteen days, remarried a year later, and divorced again after a few months. I did mention he was a lawyer, didn't I? A few years later, at his son's wedding, to which we were invited, he danced with his first ex-wife and called us a few days later to invite us to a small wedding. He and his first wife were getting married again.

It would not be wise to consider Danny as a potential husband or even as a serious potential significant other. He was far too unreliable and could not be trusted in any of those roles - bad track record. However he turned out to be just fine as a trusted friend - particularly if one was interested in finding out just what single life in one's mid 50s was all about. And so we began to explore.

The husband of one of my friends was an avowed voyeur. He suggested to us that we try a weekend at an adult camp somewhere in the Catskill Mountains called Su Casa, and so we went. The place was very basic; small rooms, mattress on floor, cubbies for clothes, hooks on doors, bathrooms on the floor, cafeteria style dining hall, paper plates, and plastic service. Not exactly the Concord or Grossinger's, but it was an adventure. We got into bathing suits and went down to the pool area where most of the other guests seemed to be congregated. This was the moment of truth and we were very overdressed. Danny had no problem; he immediately dropped his swim trunks and was appropriate for the situation. He was in tune with everyone else. That kind of body confidence did not come as easily to me but after a few awkward minutes I bit the bullet, dropped my suit, and slipped into the pool. If you have never had the delicious free feeling of skinny dipping, particularly in mixed company, you have missed one of life's delights, but on with the saga. Hanging out in the pool under the blanket of water was easy, people were very sociable and we were all in the same boat, so to speak. I was doing just fine for a while and then the gnawing worry about how in the world I was going to get out of the pool started.

Athletics is not one of my strong suits. There was no way I could lift myself out of the pool along the side nor would I if I could. That would be far too revealing. Just picture it. My only option was to walk to the shallow end of the pool and walk up the steps and in my birthday suit I had a little confidential chat with myself. I was, after all, still wearing several gold chains around my neck. I would pretend I was wearing an evening dress adorned by my gold chains. I sucked in my belly, lifted my head, looked straight ahead and walked out of the pool as if it were an everyday occurrence. We dressed and went to dinner, whereupon a whole other world opened to us.

By the time I was twenty-three I thought I was pretty sophisticated. While all of my friends whose husbands or boyfriends were in the military were living at home with their mothers, I had traveled by myself all over the country to live near my husband's army base. However, when I was suddenly single at fifty-three, I realized what interesting corners of life I knew nothing about, but I was about to find out. By nature I am a curious person, always hungry to learn new things and this was a golden opportunity. My new best friend Danny and I were on the cusps of entering a world we had never experienced.

It was approaching dinnertime at Su Casa. All of the guests were nicely dressed and lounging around on a lovely terrace on this beautiful evening. A young man was strumming a guitar and singing rather romantic songs. Most of the guests appeared to be in their thirties or forties. We were surely the oldest people there until a man and woman arrived and elected to sit near us and engage in conversation. They were of our generation and both spoke with German accents, somewhat peppered with Israeli undertones, which turned out to be their heritage. We were given our dinner camp style on disposable service and then enjoyed some dancing after which we called it a night. The next morning we left early to go antiquing and got back around noon. Most of the guests were lounging around on the lawns waiting for lunch and there were our new friends from the night before, Eric and Joan.

We joined them and Danny asked, rather jokingly whether or not there had been any "Gang Bangs" the night before. This expression was new to me but I figured it out whereupon one of the young men told us that had only been one; five guys and three girls. This activity was, of course, by mutual consent.

To my total amazement, Joan quipped, "Five guys? I could handle them by myself."

I thought surely she was being facetious so when we went in to lunch and sat together, I asked her whether or not she was joking and she assured me she was not, as her husband looked on smiling in approval. This woman was easily my age and far more matronly in appearance than I was, but she obviously knew things and walked in a world that I knew nothing about. My innocence was about to be shattered.

We entered the large carpeted room with carpeted benched seats and I quickly glanced around at the twenty or thirty people who were there. I knew why we were there, but who were all of these other people and why were they there? As we sat down the lights were somewhat dimmed, but I still could observe some of the other observers who were seated near us. To my left was a foursome of French speaking people. It would appear that they were two married couples inasmuch as they were all wearing wedding rings, but in that environment one takes nothing for granted. They were probably in their late thirties or early forties. The fellow seated next to me was very good looking. He was wearing a pair of swim trunks – bikini trunks which were not commonly seen in our country in 1975, but as I said he was French. We all waited kind of breathlessly to see what was going to happen next now that the whole group had assembled. At this point the woman who had organized the party came into the room and asked for a volunteer. "Frenchy" immediately volunteered, and instructed, placed himself on his stomach on the floor. We were now going to be taught how to give a man a sensual massage.

There was nothing new at this point except that "Frenchy" had taken off his bikini and the masseuse was astride his back. I noticed that he had a small white towel near his face and appeared to be wiping his face with it. She now had him roll over and proceeded to massage his front pretending not to notice his huge erection, and finally the dénouement. She slithered down his body she proceeded to perform fellatio on him. Although she worked vigorously he maintained his erection and finally she called that demonstration over. She knew something Danny and I did not know. Danny kept whispering to me that he could not understand how that guy didn't orgasm, but then we learned that the white powder was the culprit. He wasn't wiping his face; he was snorting a drug to prevent it from happening until he wanted it to happen.

Now the fellow who was tending bar came into the room and asked for a woman volunteer. Immediately a plain, rather matronly looking woman presented herself to him. She was wearing an eyelet beach coat ankle length. It was the sort of thing one bought on the beach in Acapulco and she was wearing it buttoned from throat to bottom. She looked like a very proper elementary schoolteacher or a bank clerk, but so much for looks. Some of the people had left the area, including the French group and when the next demonstration began, we slipped out. Once she disrobed with her voluminous floppy breasts and chunky body we had seen enough. Besides, there was more to explore. What was that back room all about?

We eyed the pool in the next room and the buffet of food, and although having had no dinner and we were hungry, first things first. We advanced to the back room, pushed aside the beads covering the entrance and holding on to the wall for it was pretty dark in there, made our way to a similar arrangement of low carpeted seating. At this point I thought

I was ready for anything, but the scene was pretty shocking. There were mats or perhaps thin mattresses all around on the floor and there were writhing bodies on them. By now our eyes had adjusted to the dark and we could see that there were couples, there were threesomes of all kinds and there were the "Frenchies," all four of them, completely entangled with each other, and anything one can imagine was happening. There was moaning, there was groaning, there was laughing, there was crying and there were sounds I cannot properly describe. With respect to one's sensibilities I leave the rest to the imagination. I had lost interest, but Danny had not so I took my leave of him for a short while. When I entered the next room, which was deserted, the pool looked so inviting that I slipped out of my clothes and into the pool. Within moments I had company. It was, of all people, "Frenchy." He swam over to me and suggested to me that I accompany him into the back room.

I smiled and said, "Not now."

He then said to me, very soulfully, "I can make you very happy."

I thanked him and again said not now. Somebody at Su Casa had clued me in that was the way to refuse and not insult the person making the offer. He graciously said goodnight and went back into the back room. I quickly got out of the pool and put on my clothes. At that point, as we approached the buffet, people started coming out of the massage room and the back room. As we were partaking of the food, a married couple we had met came over to us and greeted us as if we were at an ordinary cocktail party. When I asked them how come they were there, they told us that the sex was highly enhanced when there were other people around whom they might be watching or who might be watching them. They also told us that they frequently went to Su Casa, brought their own tent, and had wonderful sexual experiences with multiple partners.

We came, we saw, we left and laughed all the way home.

Being a people watcher, I have often appraised a seemingly unsuited looking couple and wondered, for example, why is that tall handsome guy with that unattractive ordinary looking woman? That summer of being single I found out. Moving around in the single world there were many women younger than I, richer than I, prettier than I, but somehow or other, whenever I was in mixed company someone (and sometimes more than one) would ask to see me again. I had adopted the philosophy of an experienced previously single woman about dating. It didn't matter if a guy was or was not tall, good looking, seemingly well off or brilliant. As long as he wasn't an absolute dud, a slob, morbidly obese or a depressed loser, I would give him a chance, and if he was very nervous on the first date and he asked, I would give him another chance.

That single season, from May to December I went out with eleven different men, remained friends with a few and became engaged to my soon to be second husband in December. However I must say that with the exception of one jerk, they were all gentlemen and never tried to push me sexually. The one jerk got the immediate bum's rush and was never seen or heard from again. All of this was in spite of my head full of gray hair. Whatever the signal was, I seemed to have *it* that season, and the men just flocked to it.

Throughout the summer Danny was very much on the scene. The week after our wild night in the city, Danny got a phone call from Joan. This was the German Israeli woman we had met at Su Casa, the wife of Eric, she who had scoffed when she heard of a five to three gang bang, bragging that she could handle five men herself. She called to invite us to join her and Eric for a weekend at an adult camp in Pennsylvania. We agreed to go willingly, knowing full well that we were in for a new experience. I again made it very clear to Danny that his behavior was not to be inhibited by my presence, but that in no way would I agree to partake. Whatever we would be exposed to, I was only there to look. He, of course, was in total agreement inasmuch as he was probably just as intimidated as I was.

We arrived at the camp in the early evening and were assigned to a room in a building that had about eight accommodations. All of the people in our place knew each other, including Joan and Eric. They had arranged to have dinner together and a lovely table was set for us European style, on the lawn. This proved to be fascinating. These seemed to be perfectly ordinary normal middle aged people. There were professionals, business people, educators, all stripes of life, and they were all swingers. Conversation around the table ranged anywhere from front page to the arts, just as it would around my dining room table at a dinner party. My curiosity quotient was overwhelmed and when one of the women left the table to go to the euphemism I immediately joined her.

She was a very lovely looking woman, late forties or thereabout and her husband was well built and good looking. I took the bull by the horns and asked her if she could tell me, the neophyte, what this was all about and how she became involved. She told me that her husband owns a large marina that accommodates many yachts. One of his customers was a very attractive wealthy divorcee with a teenage son. She wanted to take the boat down to Florida but wanted to take a leisurely cruise. Her son and cook would join them and she wanted this woman's husband to captain the yacht. Over her rather meek protests he opted to go.

During the winter there was some major problem with the yacht so he had to fly to Florida to accommodate his client and she understood that the client needed attention not the yacht. When he returned she initiated a heart to heart discussion and they both agreed that life had gotten somewhat boring and both were looking for some excitement. What was the route to take to save their marriage was swinging. How does one go about finding swingers, the clarion of all things weird, *The Village Voice*? Just look under "Swingers" and you will find various clubs.

The first night of discovery ended rather uneventfully,

that is uneventfully for Danny and me. We had no idea what may or may not have happened after we bid goodnight to the group, but we were ready to call it a night. We were sure that we would get first-hand information from our friends Eric and Joan the following day, and right we were.

The following morning our friends invited us to have breakfast with them, which we eagerly did. After all, this was a learning experience and we knew that our mentors were our new friends.. To say we were curious would be an understatement, so at breakfast I asked Joan to tell us what this whole thing was about. How it operated and how they became involved; two such seemingly, almost conservative people. And so, the story unfurled.

Eric started bringing home copies of *The Village Voice*. This was not their usual daily newspaper, *The New York Times* and Eric seemed consumed with a particular section. She sensed that this was something serious for Eric, and so she asked to be included in his fantasies. He showed her the variety of ads for Swinger Clubs, of which there were many in New York and they decided to investigate. The first time at a club they were struck by how "normal" the people appeared to be. They looked like any group of business people who had stopped by for a drink after work or before dinner. Our friends sidled up to the bar next to a very attractive couple who they found to be very friendly and talkative. They were informed that there were very strict rules in this society. This was strictly a couples situation and private arrangement would be a violation and not to be tolerated. After a period of small talk, they all agreed that they were compatible and set a date for a future meeting. The man was an airline pilot and his partner was a head "stewardess," which was how they were known as in 1976, and they were both very attractive.

At the appointed time the couple arrived at Joan's apartment in Forest Hills. Tea was served inasmuch as both Eric and Joan did not approve of alcoholic beverages. After some light conversation, the pilot invited Joan into her bedroom and Eric invited the stewardess into the guest room. They all proceeded to enjoy sex. These were the proper rules of engagement. When everyone was completely satisfied, the guests dressed, arranged a future date to be held at their apartment, and left.

Eric and Joan were very happy that this initial meeting turned out so well and they anxiously looked forward to the next experience. The second meeting turned out differently.

The procedure was the same but the end result was not. This is how Joan put it. The couples were fine and the sex was great but the apartment was not neat and clean. They knew that they could not be involved with that couple again. What kind of homemaker does not have a neat clean apartment when she invites guests over? How can you be expected to have nice comfortable sex in that environment? Danny and I exchanged covert glances at each other. Each of us was trying to figure out how it was possible to have sex with a total stranger but to be turned off by an apartment that was not Good Housekeeping clean. Obviously we had a great more to learn.

Getting back to the camp, by now it was very clear what this was all about. These were adults who considered overt sexual activity as accepted social behavior. This behavior was as normal to them as my social behavior was to me, like movies, theater, cultural events or dinner with another couple or two. Less frequent might be dinner and dancing. The furthest I would go was perhaps dancing with someone's male guest; maybe even flirting or snuggling on the dance floor, but red flags went up at that point. Sometimes an evening of carousing and dancing might invite a Monday morning phone call suggesting "doing lunch" which of course had other connotations. That was amusing, even flattering, but certainly laughed off and never accepted. If anything it felt inappropriate.

"That's very tempting but you know my husband," I would say. I had a stock replied worked out. "He would find out and he would kill us both." That ended that. I had a very persistent brother-in-law and laughingly I would tell him that he knew my husband's keen intuition from which we could never escape. We would be so nervous that we would probably have a car accident, and if we didn't get killed he would finish the job. It remained a joke between us but when he found out that I was dating Danny he was very offended. Why Danny and not him? He tended to forget that not only was he married, but he was married to my late husband's sister. Admittedly there are all kinds of social morals, but dating married men was off my chart.

Regarding social morals, I was far from naïve at that point but the norm at the camp was mind boggling. Nudity, of course was accepted, but public sexual activity was beyond my realm of expectation. I leave the details to the reader's imagination and wherever that imagination takes you is not beyond the probable. The hottest place, both literally and figuratively, was a huge hot tub in a separate building. Those who came here and sat around the rim of the tub were open for anything. The lights were dim and the action was astounding. The tub was pretty large, large enough for a short swim. The swimmers would just swim over to someone who was sitting around the rim, short conversation or no conversation, and perform oral sex. This was a bit much for me and I slithered out of the building with Danny right in back of me. It was not evening and we sat around with drinks, chatted with some of the people who were not otherwise engaged and called it a night.

The next day was our last day there. We were lounging on the lawn and wanted to have some wine, which was in our room. We flipped a coin; I lost so I had to go up to get the bottle. My room was opposite Joan and Eric's. As I was leaving my room Joan's door opened and a fellow came out. A quick glance showed three or four other men involved with Joan on the bed and Eric sitting on the windowsill watching. I was paralyzed but the door closed quickly and nobody saw me standing there. I snapped out of my trance and ran down to tell Danny what I had just witnessed. Apparently when

Joan told us at Su Casa that she was unimpressed with a five guy three gal gang bang, she meant it. Even though I heard it from her and I saw it with my own eyes, I was still having trouble believing it.

It was soon time to go home and back to reality. That weekend at the camp was like a forbidden step into the dark side of life.

A few weeks after the camp, as a joke I called Danny imitating Joan's accent. I was sure he would recognize a hoax, but he didn't. A few days later he called me and told me that he was in a phone booth across the street from Joan's apartment. He had called her and indicated that he was interested in seeing her. She was receptive and invited him up. Eric was at work and the bedroom was available. So much for living by the rules of the swingers. This woman was indeed a free soul and Danny was learning how to be one.

We had no contact with Eric and Joan for several months and my life's path changed direction. Danny and I were still friends but we were no longer dating inasmuch as I had committed myself to marry Stan. And then, something amazing happened. Eric and Joan's daughter became engaged to the son of Danny's close friend. There was to be an engagement party at this friend's home and we were invited. Joan called Danny, terrified. Her daughter, a practicing psychologist, had absolutely no idea of her parents' lifestyle as nudists, let alone swingers. As I had said previously, these were Germans who had migrated to Israel and then on to the U.S. It is not unusual for people to look for opportunities to be with people of similar background and their daughter was under the impression that the camp in Pennsylvania that her parents frequented was one such place. Her parents were apartment dwellers and the premise was that they enjoyed the outdoors, biking, hiking and being with fellow German Jews. There was no reason to think otherwise.

The next time we saw them was at the engagement party. To strangers, they seemed to be a very staid, respectable almost old fashioned rather matronly couple. Their personal presentation appeared remarkably normal. We greeted each other cordially, as if we were occasional bridge players and they understood that their secret was safe with us. We never saw them again and although our relationship with them was really short lived it was certainly very intense and quite an education.

There was one after-effect to that incredible summer.

A very close friend, a family physician, had moved with family, to California. They were coming to New York for vacation. He had become a sex therapist, dealing in reality treatment with patients suffering with sexual dysfunction. His story was that he wanted to go to Plato's Retreat strictly as an observer of course. This would enhance his expertise and help him help his patients. The problem was that Plato's was not accessible to unaccompanied males. Women could come in unescorted but not men. He asked me if I would go with him. What? Forget that, but I could ask Danny. Sure enough Danny was willing and able to come up with two agreeable females and so they went. His wife spent the evening with us around a piano bar at a single's place and we all looked forward to brunch the next morning when he would tell us about his experience.

How he had the guts to admit to us in the company of his wife that he was not only an observer but also an active participant blew my mind. His report was that the women were so aggressive with creative sex that there was no way to stay out of it. It is hard to judge the dynamics of someone else's marriage and there is much to be said about this particular marriage, but that's another story.

The transition from wife to widow to single woman did not happen magically. I was filled with fear, the overwhelming one of which was the fear of being alone. I was again a child afraid of the dark, afraid of being alone at night. What if something unexpected or unforeseen happened? What if I felt sick and there was nobody there to help me? I could die alone in that big house and nobody would be there to help me. Fears do not require reality or reason. The fact that I had traveled and lived alone during the army years when Que was in the States was obliterated by the emotional damage visited upon me during Que's overseas war years. Although unbeknownst to me my fragile emotional stability was always a challenge. My agoraphobic gremlins always lurked nearby, ready to tease me and there was no Que around to protect me.

Aunt Sadie, quietly sensitive to my needs, stayed with me for a few weeks and together we went to Florida. All of my aunts and uncles were living there. One night we gathered at one of their homes. I really loved them, but seeing them all together, enjoying their lives, erupted a deep rooted never before articulated emotion.

"How did you do what you did to me?" I asked tearfully.

They looked at me, confused. I was a ten year old child and somebody told me that I was going to live with my Bubby now. How was I supposed to know who my Bubby was? I had lived a charade from as far back as I could remember thinking my stepmother was my mother and I had no idea who that generous old lady was who came once or twice a year and who brought gifts. Not one of them thought to explain to a ten year old child whose father had just died that the old woman was my mother's mother, that she loved my sister and me, and that she wanted us. I was torn away from my family as I knew it and put into a new strange environment without a word of explanation.

"Would any one of you do that to your children?" They were all stunned and couldn't look at me.

Finally, my Uncle Morris, dear sweet man that he was, sadly said to me, "We were so busy trying to survive; it never occurred to us that we were hurting you. That was surely never our intention."

There was nothing left to be said, and for me it was a catharsis and a turning point of some sort. I had unwittingly gotten rid of a festering hurt.

Sadie had injured her foot while in Florida and when

we got back, her son Jerry picked her up and took her to his home and my son Bobby picked me up at the airport. He had come prepared to spend the night, but I was feeling prepared to face my reality. I reassured both myself and my son and insisted that he go home. The clock in my head told me that it was time to move on but I really didn't quite know how. At fifty-three, I was the only one of my friends who had lost her husband and I had no idea what to expect. Wendy's best friend Ann's father had died a few months before and one day her mother Harriet, who I knew casually, paid a visit. It was an opportunity for me to someone of comparative age who was in my situation. After we chatted about the girls, who were living together in Denver, I asked her how she handled it.

What she told me was not very encouraging, quite disheartening in fact. She said, "Five days a week, I go to my office at the bank. While there I'm all right. I come home at the end of the day, have something to eat, and try to watch some TV, and end up crying myself to sleep".

"What about weekends?" I asked, afraid to hear the answer.

"Once a month I go out with my group of married

friends. Sometimes my son comes to visit. Other than that, it's the same as during the week. I am home alone."

When she left I knew I had to prepare a different scenario for myself but did not yet know how. And then, Bebe came into my life.

Bebe

Bebe was a woman who I knew very casually. We moved in the same large social circle but really had no more than a nod and smile relationship. She was married to a very dynamic man, or so I was given to understand. He was National Vice President of the Letter Carriers Union, and was the president of the New York and Puerto Rico branches. This all translated into being a lobbyist in Washington, D.C. which sounded pretty prestigious, and I was intrigued the first time I met him.

It was a winter weekend at the Nevele Hotel in the Catskills, a fundraising project for Hadassah and a large group of us went. Several of us, after seeing the Late Show, the risqué Late show, and gone tobogganing were gathered in the Coffee Shop to warm up with hot chocolates. It was about 3 a.m. and this attractive, albeit balding fellow stood up on one of the tables and in the most mellifluous voice made the following proclamation: "Ladies and gentlemen, friends, we have partaken in all of the amenities that this hotel has offered us, and now that there is nothing left to do, let us retire to our rooms and fuck our wives."

I must say that in that era, we were a bit more cautious about using that language publicly, but it wasn't so much what he said, but rather the way he said it in that beautiful voice of his and his commanding presence. To my mind this was someone to reckon with.

To me, Bebe, who I barely knew through Hadassah, was a rather benign looking person with nothing that attracted me to want to develop a friendship, but her husband Phil, wow. A few weeks later we were surprised to be invited to a party at their home and were pleased to accept. That spring we reciprocated by inviting them to a party at our home and shortly afterwards they moved from Bayswater to a new home in Atlantic Beach, where they had a lovely large housewarming party. When the group dwindled quite late that evening, some of us, the remaining diehards, were all lounging in the living room. I was sitting on the floor when Phil reclined on the floor next to me.

We were chatting about this and that and as Que and I prepared to leave, Phil said to me, "Talking to you is like reading the Sunday New York Times after reading the Daily News all week."

I was blown away by the flattery. The next morning, before I had a chance to call our hostess and thank her for a lovely evening, she called me and said, "I had the best sex with my husband last night. It's a good thing he did not mention your name."

We both had a good laugh over it. That was Bebe as I knew her at that time. We could not possibly imagine as we kidded around about her husband those two weeks later he would succumb to a massive heart attack. He was fifty-two years old.

In the next several months, we would frequently get a phone call on a late Sunday morning. She would be having a "come as you are" soiree and we would get together with her and a few other friends. By the end of that year, or thereabout, Bebe dropped out of my life.

The next time I saw her was five years later. Que had

just died and she paid the traditional Shiva call. She stayed a very short time and she said to me, "You don't need me now, you are surrounded by people. I will come back to see you when you will need me." I did not realize at the time how astute that was. She did come back about three months later, with her gentleman friend, insisting that I have lunch with them. That afternoon was an eye opener for me.

Bebe's gentleman friend was Fred. I was invited to go with her and Fred to lunch and a movie. However, in the restaurant sitting at the table with them, I knew pretty early on that the movie idea was doomed. They were so into each other, flirting, smiling, restrained touching, and a not too subtle suggestion of sex. I discreetly old them that although it was delightful sharing lunch with them, I would absent myself and skip the "movie." They made the appropriate objections but I was sure they were anxious to be alone.

As time passed, I learned that although Fred was married, he and Bebe had been lovers for several months. That he was married seemed of no consequence to him and was a positive issue for her. He and his wife owned an apartment in Long Beach, but she preferred Florida and stayed there most of the time. It was a perfect setup.

Time went on and I learned that Fred owned a flourishing business in New York, had plenty of money and enjoyed total freedom. I was surprised when Bebe told me that he bought her expensive clothes, but when she told me that he gave her cash every week I was astounded. I did not want to look at her romance for what it really was. Since her house in Atlantic Beach was rented to a bunch of airline stewardesses for the summer, she was now living with me and that arrangement sat well with me. My loneliness was somewhat assuaged by her presence in my home, as my delight grew to find that there could be life and love after the loss of a spouse.

Bebe had her own philosophy about men. Although she was a single woman she was not interested in single men. She liked married discontent men who demanded nothing of her except great sex and playfulness. They were not looking for a future, for marriage, for responsibility, or anything of that nature. As she explained to me, she had no conscience about taking money from them.

"After all," she said to me one day when I questioned her about that, "If they take up my time they have to take care of me." She was monogamous, one man at a time, but the reality was that I had opened my home and had accepted friendship from a whore. It really was none of my business and I chose not to condemn anything.

In the late fall of that year her bubble burst. Someone alerted Mrs. Fred of his infidelity. How she didn't realize that by living apart as they did made their marriage vulnerable to this kind of thing seems pretty stupid. However the alert did not go unheeded. She came home without advising him and of course he was not there. He was out with Bebe and when he came home, rumpled and with the scent of her perfume on his person "Mrs. Fred" swallowed a large amount of pills. It was a suicide drama but it was enough to close the book on the Bebe and Fred saga Fred's name now had a new appendage. From that day on he was referred to as "Fucking Fred."

Bebe was devastated. She had delusions that this affair had roots. She was pretty naïve for an experienced woman. This was far from her first affair with a married man. Invariably they ended up the same way. All of them, that is, except the last one.

It is not my intention to create the impression that Bebe was a bad person; she was not. Her perspective on life was just different from mine. On the surface one could say that she was using me, my home, and my loneliness to satisfy her needs. She was but obviously she was helping me work through my own darkness. Our symbiosis was in harmony.

She cried her way through the next few months. The flight attendants who had rented her home went back to wherever they came from and so her house was empty. However, she was mourning the loss of F. Fred and was immobilized. She just could not go back to what she now referred to as their love-nest. That was a stretch in as much as she did not have access to the house for the last few months of their affair. I cannot know for sure whether it was the man, the affair or the compensation but whatever it was it was real for her and she was having a hard time dealing with it.

At this time I had become involved with a wonderful man, Stan, with whom I was soon to become engaged. Life had taken a remarkable turn and one could infer that Bebe and I had changed places from the day that she walked into my life with F. Fred. Now she was deeply unhappy but *I* was basking in the sunshine of life. My future was nice and bright.

A few days before Christmas, my friendly neighbor invited us to a major Christmas party at the Puck Building, a most popular venue for events of that sort. My fiancé was out of town and I wanted to go, but not alone. It took a great deal of pushing and prodding and I convinced Bebe to go with me, a most fortuitous decision. It was a real New York kind of event sponsored by one of the very large advertising agencies for their important clients.

Although I acted as though this was a normal occurrence in my life I was really impressed by the grandness of it. Coming out of the elevator we found ourselves in a broad foyer. On either end there was a large ballroom teaming with bodies dancing to the music of live orchestras. Each ballroom had a large bar and handsomely outfitted good looking young men serving wonderful small foods. This was a serious cocktail party and there was some pretty serious drinking and carousing going on. Flirting and propositioning was the main course.

Moments after we arrived I found myself being escorted to the bar by a very attractive, nicely put together fellow. We each had a martini, made some small talk, did some slow dancing, had another martini and then were among the undulating bodies on the dance floor. The Hustle was the popular dance of the day, and we did hustle. This guy was handsome, he was hot and he sure could dance. The situation could have become a little hard to handle but fortunately he had to leave early to catch a flight to Florida where his wife and children were vacationing. As he was leaving he handed me his card on the back of which he had written his return flight information, urging me to meet him on his return. I played along with it knowing that my fiancé and I were going to Mexico that weekend. It was fun and he was an experienced roué. I doubt he took me seriously.

When he left I began to look for Bebe. We had made eye contact several times on the dance floor and I knew she was holding her own. My search was cut very short by another man asking me to dance. That's basically what one does at this kind of party. One is either drinking or dancing or both and so it was back on the dance floor for me. This guy tried, he really did but he was no match for his predecessor. In fact he was a dud, but a seemingly nice gentleman. I decided to introduce him to Bebe and to investigate the other ballroom before leaving. She was standing speaking to two men. I think they were father and son and they were working their points very animatedly. I signaled her to come over to me which she did and suggested that she dance with Bob. I went to check out the other room, Bebe danced with Bob and life would never be the same for them.

In 1976 there were no laws about drunk driving. We had never heard of DWI, DUI, breath tests or the like. If we had, neither one of us would have qualified to drive home. At any rate when we approached Bebe's car, she advised me in no uncertain terms that she was in no shape to drive home. It was up to me and I had no choice. Driving home was all I could do to keep my eyes open. When we spotted a Carvel as we got off the highway I was grateful to keep myself awake with the cold treat. On the way home, she kept telling me that this old guy who I had introduced to her wanted her to meet him in Garden City. It went something like this:

"I would like to see you after the holidays. I'm busy with my family but really would like to see you."

"Well, maybe."

"Do you ever come to Garden City?"

"I shop at Saks all of the time."

"Great, we can do lunch. Here is my card. Please call me."

"He thinks I'll call him," Bebe informed me. "Hm, he seems pretty old and dull to me. Here is his card. I can't read it. I don't have my glasses. What does it say?"

"Don't show me his card now," I told her. "I can hardly keep my eyes open, let alone drive your damned car. We'll look at it later."

When we got home, I went to my answering machine to see if my fiancé had called me, which he had, and she went looking for her glasses. She came tearing into the room all excited, "Look at this, look at this!" She shouted, "This is quite a guy!"

I looked at the card. It read "Robert Fielding, Senior Vice President Roosevelt Savings Bank." Now that was impressive! Suddenly he didn't look so old and Bebe was absolutely interested. This guy had the qualifications of a good catch. He was obviously well off and he was married. The wheels in Bebe's head started turning.

Christmas holidays came and went and Bebe's scheme went into action. "Doing lunch" as the expression goes among cheaters is the first step. I knew that expression because sometimes the day after a wild party I would get a phone call from some friend's husband asking me to meet in the city to "Do lunch." Frankly, I never had the desire, and even if I did, I never had the guts. But Bebe knew the vernacular better than I and she was ready for it. So lunch it was and a subsequent date to visit her at my house the next day while I was at work. I must admit that there was some vicarious excitement for me about her forthcoming escapade and when I left for work the next morning I made her promise me that she would share every detail with me. She was perfectly willing.

About two hours after I left I got a phone call from her. She told me that she went to a lingerie shop in Cedarhurst and bought herself a white peignoir set. She lit a fire in the fireplace in the living room and made a makeshift bed, sheets and pillows in front of the fireplace and was waiting for him. This lady knew how to handle a man. As we spoke, I heard the doorbell ring at my front door and I knew that Bob has arrived.

I didn't quite know how to feel. He was married so that wasn't right, but then again it was their lives not mine and I could feel the electricity in the air, even over the phone. I was going to be witness to a new experience. My friend the whore was at work.

I put Bebe's saga out of my mind at work, but driving home I was wondering how this would play out. Was she going to be able to put F. Fred out of her life and take up with another married man? It was as risky as walking into a minefield with one's eyes wide open, but then again this was the pattern of her life since her husband died. Oh, did I mention that she had an affair with her best friend's husband for thirteen years while they both were married? Did I mention that her eight year old daughter walked in on them one day when school let out early? And did I mention that "Mr. Best Friend's" husband came to Bebe's house every night during the mourning period to join a minyan for prayers and then he dropped her the day it was over? This played havoc with her daughters' mind, but that's a whole other story.

When I arrived home I found a euphoric Bebe waiting for me. She proceeded to detail the events. When Bob arrived he was carrying a package, "What do you think was in it?" she asked.

Knowing what his mission was I responded questioningly, "A robe?"

She burst out laughing for in fact that it was. She then proceeded to tell me that he also had a bottle of chilled champagne. She went upstairs and drew a bath for him and served him champagne in the bathtub while he luxuriated in the warm bubbles sipping the cold bubbles and enjoying her generously endowed body. She did know how to treat a man. I told her that she was born much too late. She would have fared well as a courtesan in an earlier century.

From the onset we had a lot of fun. Bebe recovered from her trauma over the loss of F. Fred and after a short time she returned home to her love nest, but with a different lover. Bob became a three evening visitor but never a sleepover guest. I don't know if he knew the rules inasmuch as he was quite a roué or if Bebe taught them to him right up front, "If he is going to take up my time, he is going to take care of me." Those were the rules and he stood by them. He gave her money every week.

Stan and I were engaged by the time we came home from Mexico and he, Bebe, and I lived together until she moved out. We had a favorite restaurant, Tavernetta in Woodmere, and we were there every Friday night. They had a piano player, an elderly black gay gentleman who knew all of the songs that we liked. As soon as the four of us walked in he would start playing "The Second Time Around" and we would virtually dance into the bar, a very active scene.

In his position at the bank, Bob had access to a few

very classy restaurants in the city, which was very nice for us since we were his guests as he was the guest of certain special clients. Life was good, but like all things, change happens.

Bob had a family, a wife and three grown children. Of course one always wonders why people stray and yet stay married. Bob's story was that his wife was an alcoholic and drank and collapsed on the sofa every evening. When he discussed with her the fact that he had certain needs and she had certain conjugal obligations she just sweetly advised him that if he needed sex he was welcome to go out and find it. She was not interested in sex or divorce.

At this time Bebe and Bob were both about sixty years old. From the time he was sixteen years old he had worked for the bank with a furlough for military service. He was already married with one child when drafted and he had the good fortune to go to officer training school and become an officer. His good fortune was further enhanced by an assignment in Washington, D.C. for the duration of the war, where he had something to do with writing articles regarding analyzing army food. I must admit to having forgotten the details but it was some kind of benign nonsense job. After the war he returned to the same bank and proceeded to have two more children, all of whom were adults when this new romance began.

Valerie, the eldest, was single, beautiful, and had been a face model in Paris. She was in a relationship with a gentleman who was twenty five years her senior, married to an ailing wife, and quite rich. He was a music publisher who had a few songs of his own that were quite popular. Next was Mitchell; married, two sons, and well on the road to great success professionally. Then there was Jerold, a lovely gentle boy who was somewhat mentally challenged. Today he would probably be classified as Asperger's but at the time it was unknown. He was just slow and lived at home.

Bebe had two children. She always insisted she did not know how she became

pregnant with Herbert at seventeen. She claimed that all she did was sit on Phil's lap. She undoubtedly did, didn't she? Well, in that era, seventeen and pregnant led to marriage even though he was also seventeen, still in high school, and only had a part time job at the post office. Her next child, Katie was ten years younger, all while having had an abortion here and there in the interim. I was not privy to the reason for that. Anyway, both of her offspring were married with three children apiece.

These descriptions would hardly set the scene for a hot romance, but that's what it became. Shortly after they enjoyed that fateful bathtub scene, Bob advised Bebe that he was going to California on business. Nothing special about that except that he had invited a lady friend to accompany him. The arrangement had been made before he met Bebe and he perceived himself too much of a gentleman to disappoint the lady. However, to relieve Bebe of any unhappiness, he suggested that instead of flying home from California, he would send the lady back alone. He would feign sudden unexpected business in Florida, and Bebe could meet him there for a cruise. This guy was not about to miss an opportunity that had the scent of pleasure. She deliberated.

"How can I go on a cruise with him?" she whined to me.

"Are you kidding?" I queried. "Are you trying to tell me that you are suddenly shy?"

"No, not that silly," she answered. "You know I'm not shy about my body. But those bathrooms are right in the cabin and what if I have to have a BM. I can be pretty noisy"

"So, my dear. When you get the call of the wild, just ask him to leave the cabin. And by the way, he's human also.

You know you are going, so cut the dramatics." (Or did I say *cut the bullshit?* Probably)

Of course she went. They met at a hotel in Florida for a few days and went on the cruise. She related to me afterwards that one night he wanted to stay at the bar and she wanted to go to bed so he escorted her back to the cabin and returned to the bar. This did not sit to well with her, so she put on a loose fitting blouse minus bra, went to the bar, lifted up her blouse, revealed her generous breasts to all who were looking and returned to the cabin. Of course he followed and the rest can play out in your imagination.

After the cruise they returned to the hotel in Florida. He called his office and extended his leave. He was, after all, a senior vice president and as that could pretty much do whatever the spirit moved him to do. He also called his wife and explained to her where he was and told her that business required a few more days away. He just didn't advise her about what kind of business. This last call set the scene for trouble. They were staying there for four more days and on the fourth morning wife Andrea called to confirm Bob's arrival time the afternoon. This was Bebe's chance. She had agreed not to answer the phone, if it rang. But Bob was sleeping and she grabbed the phone. Her excuse was that she didn't want to wake him; a pretty thin excuse. Anyway, Bob heard the phone, took it from her and babbled some kind of nonsense about housekeeping coming early. He was satisfied that he had covered his ass.

Given their arrangement, it doesn't quite fit that his wife, Andrea should care if he was there with someone. But then again everything about that whole Bob arrangement didn't fit. I now started to figure it out and came to the conclusion that it was okay for him to have his dalliances, but not anything serious that would threaten her marriage. You see, Andrea also had her rules.

Now it became a silent though very definite battle. Andrea knew who the enemy was; she had found the receipt of Bebe's flight trip to and from Florida on Bob's dresser, with Bebe's name on it. Was this an accident on Bob's part or did he want to be found out and to have a confrontation with Andrea? He would never admit to that; it was too much a sign of weakness. Nevertheless, Bob now found himself the pawn in a battle between a drunk and a whore.

The drunk would not put out but also would not let go. The whore was in a stronger position. She had experience, she knew what she wanted and she knew that she was pretty much in control because Bob was a very sexual man and Bebe had no boundaries.

Life settled into a pattern for a while. Bob saw Bebe three nights a week and gave her money weekly. I wish I could have been a fly on the wall when she negotiated that deal. I never could figure out how a woman asks a man for money for her favors. But she did. Once in a while something would come up and she would pressure him for a Saturday night and somehow he would manage. But when she pushed him to stay overnight one Saturday night, Andrea pushed the red button. Sunday morning Bebe got a phone call asking for Bob. It was Andrea. Although Bebe knew she was in control of Bob she nevertheless got nervous at the sound of Andrea's voice. Bob took the call and then told Bebe that he had to go home. His three children had congregated at his home in support of their mother and demanded that he appear for a showdown.

When he got home, they were in fact all there. I cannot tell you what actually transpired, but I do know that at one point Andrea told Bob in no uncertain terms it was time for him to make a decision. It was one thing for him to whore around, but quite another for him to have a paid mistress. The cards were on the table. Andrea knew everything about his "sordid affair" and it was time to make a choice. She really thought that he was not about to give up his social position of vice president of the bank with an appropriate wife for this Jewish broad in Atlantic Beach who would not be acceptable by the stuffy bank cronies. Well, he went up to the bedroom and an hour or so later, he returned with two suitcases filled with his clothing and bid his wife farewell. Once again sex trumped status.

When Bebe started to nag Bob about divorcing Andrea he made his intentions very clear. His bank contract assured that whoever was his wife up until the day he was sixty-five would be the recipient of his pension in the event of an untimely death. He felt that Andrea was entitled to that after all of the years of marriage and so no talk of divorce would be entertained until he was sixty-five. You see, Bob had his rules also.

Now Bob was a bigamist, not in any actual sense, but certainly from a practical point of view. He took care of wife number one financially, and at the same time took up family life with Bebe, supporting her as well. That was okay since he could afford it.

Little by little he started introducing her to his drinking buddies, his bank cronies. Remarkably, she managed to handle them, or so it appeared. She wasn't too popular with the women but she sure knew how to make the men feel good about themselves. Her life with Phil in his lobbying profession had prepared her and she was not intimidated by these people. She really never knew how much she didn't know.

Something remarkable happened after Bob moved out of the house. As I had mentioned Jerold, his younger son, was mildly intellectually challenged. He lived at home, had a large music collection, and stayed in his room most of the time listening to his music. He was a hermit, antisocial, and very self-conscious. He was twenty-seven years old and had never had a job. A few days after his father moved out, he sought out a Halfway House in the city. The head of the house found a part time job for him in the shipping department of a publishing company. He was educable, had gone to private schools, and even had a college degree. The publishing company had some kind of program which allowed him to go on for a Master's degree in Library Science and he became a Librarian. He qualified for a job in the New York Library System and was able to support himself thereafter. Apparently his father's decision gave him the courage to move on. That assuaged much of Bob's guilt.

After about four years, Bob turned sixty five. A week after his birthday he flew down to Mexico and got his divorce. Now there was no going back.

On Christmas day, Bebe called me and told me that they wanted to get married the next day. Would I call a friend of mine who was a judge to see if he could do the honors? He was agreeable if we could be there no later than nine o'clock the following morning. They had had the license for quite a while, so when the four of us arrived at the appointed hour the ceremony was brief, smooth, and to the point. We then went to the Sherwood Diner for a wedding breakfast. If you have read or seen the movie Dr. Jekyll and Mr. Hyde you can anticipate what is about to unfurl. Bebe had the ring and the contract. The shrew emerged. She got on Bob's back over some nonsense and let him know who the boss was in no uncertain terms.

There is much more to the story of Bebe as there is about any one of us but there is only one more item that influenced my life at that particular time. It involved my friend Jackie.

When she was a young divorcée with two small daughters, Jackie married Chris, a fine gentleman twenty years her senior. She was Jewish, he was Greek, and together they had a son. He was a loving father to all three children. The older daughter married into a Jewish Greek family. The wedding introduced me to an ethnicity with which I had never had any social intercourse and which fascinates me to this very day. These people, many of whom are related, have an organization which they call the Pashas. They are dedicated to one goal: having a good time enjoying life. And they love to dance! At all of their events, be it a wedding, a dinner dance or a simple barbeque, they have that Greek music rolling either by way of a band or a DJ, and they are on their feet dancing. Their energy seems boundless.

Periodically they take over a resort hotel band and all and the music goes in all day and into the wee hours of the night. Jackie and Chris fit right into the scene. One of those weekends occurred shortly after Stan and I became involved with each other, but not yet intimate. Jackie suggested that we come up to the Catskills, where the Pashas had taken a hotel, either for the weekend or even just for a day. It took a bit of urging and when I suggested it to Stan, he was very ready to go. We shyly agreed it would be for a day.

We had to sign in inasmuch as we would be partaking in all of the amenities and food. When we did, the room clerk innocently told us that all of the rooms in the hotel were taken but they could get us settled in a motel right across the road. Unannounced, both Stan and I had taken a small "emergency" bag and we agreed to take a motel room. The room clerk blandly advised us if we wanted "dirty movies" it would be an extra $5.00. We burst out laughing and went for that option.

Before dinner, we went to the room to relax and change clothes. When I reached into my bag to take out my negligee, I found a large soft covered book. Unbeknownst to me, Bebe had slipped it into my bag. Before we left she had given me a gold charm of two fingers crossed for good luck. But the book was a surprise. And what was the book? "All You Ever Wanted To Know About Sex But Were Too Afraid to Ask." That Bebe!

She really had set the scene for us. I took a bubble bath, Stan explored the book and the natural course of events was set into motion.

Stan, and Another Move

It's rather a personal story, but I'd like to tell you about it. It has to do with my declaration of refusal to see myself as a widow, although in fact that was what I was, and my determination to see myself as a single woman. As such, when a friend invited me to join her on a singles weekend in the mountains, I went, but with great trepidations I admit. There is much to be said about that kind of experience, but there is really only one element that is relevant to this writing. The first morning's entertainment was a palmist and after the lecture I had her read my palm. She told me some really awesome things about myself but what I want to share at this time was her recognizing that I was a single woman, not such a big trick on a singles weekend, but told me that I would not be single for two years. She also told me that I would not have to look for my future husband, that he would come to me and that I would meet him in my own backyard. The weekend progressed. I sat on many barstools, met many men, but this wasn't my own backyard, a metaphor, and these were not the important barstools.

About six weeks later I went with a friend to a local singles barbeque held in the home of one of the participants. I met a very lovely gentleman there and although I did not think he was right for me, he was gently persistent and very patient. He was just so sweet that I agreed to go to dinner with him. He was legally separated for two years and was very clear that he would never get married again. My husband had died only eight months before and I was certainly not thinking of marriage. We saw each other three times and then he went off to Paris and I continued to go out with other people. Somehow I managed to meet a lot of guys that summer. When he got back, he asked me out to dinner, and I went. There was a place called Conerrico in Cedarhurst, and it had a lovely, dimly lit lounge with a combo playing romantic music. We elected to sit on bar stools and Stan started telling me about the wonders of Paris as he saw it on that trip and how much he wished I could have been there with him. Well, he couldn't wait to take me there. This started to sound serious. He may or may not have realized it sitting there on that bar stool, but he was asking me to marry him. We were married five months later, went to Paris every time we were in Europe, which we did almost yearly, and had the most wonderful twenty-five year journey together. Until death did us part.

I have not written too much about my second husband Stan Becker because it is hard to present an almost idyllic relationship without sounding false or prone to fantasy. However, really it was beautiful. For this I take very little personal credit. It was beautiful because he was beautiful. To this day, if his name is mentioned among friends or family it is always with affectionate tenderness and frequently a bit of eye wetting. Another component in our wonderful balance was the fact that his ex-wife was such a shrew that she was not a hard act to follow. His experience with her was so distasteful in every direction that I came across as close to perfection as is humanly possible, which of course I am not. However, in my own defense I will say that I am an acknowledged spoiler of men, and who can resist being spoiled? But we are only human and as such do have our frailties.

Stan and I never had an argument in our twenty-five years of marriage. His nature was very slow to irritate and because of that I reflected in a similar way. The thought of reprimanding him if he did something that I perceived as inappropriate or frankly stupid would be beyond my ability. It would stay blocked in my mind; obliterated by the vision of a hurt look in his eyes which I could not bring myself to incur. He had many years of that in his previous life and did not deserve that from me. There was always a kinder way to get the point across and I was not interested in creating or winning arguments. Stan certainly was not. He was everlastingly grateful for the serenity in our lives.

Of course there were bumps in the road. He had two young daughters, sixteen and nineteen years old. When we met two years after the separation, they expressed how they hated the arguments between their parents and hated the way their mother treated their father, always begging him to leave and praying that he wouldn't. They told me, when we were married about five years and the girls and I had established very solid relationships with each other, that the day we were married, they each took turns in the bathroom crying. Although they wanted their father, who they adored until the day that he died, to be happy, they realized the day that their father remarried that their childhood had really ended. They would never be a family again. The whole dynamic had changed for them on that day.

About two years into our marriage, the "ex" got married, and as such was no longer eligible to receive alimony. What a relief that was. Up until then, my exact take home check was equal to her provision. Just about that time my daughter got married and I decided to invite the ex and her husband to the wedding. With that move I had created an extended family. My rationale to myself was that these two girls had suffered enough. Hopefully there would be weddings, grandchildren, holidays and many reasons that families gather for celebrations. Would it not be better for everyone if we could all be civil and spare the girls further angst worrying about whom to be with at these events? It worked out just fine. When friends heard that the ex and her husband were coming for let us say Thanksgiving and would stay at our apartment overnight since they lived out of town, they thought that I had departed from sanity. I had not. As long as Stan was not uncomfortable with the situation, I was very proud that a potential source of unhappiness for the girls had been averted and their mother and I referred to each other as sisters-out-laws. At the risk of seeming to praise myself, I will say that I had established a model plan for behavior of divorced parents putting the feelings and needs of their children above their own displeasure or hostility. Admittedly sometimes the wounds are so deep that civility is beyond the possible, but given Stan's personality and my desire for peace and tranquility, it worked beautifully for us.

Although I really loved my home, it became evident that it was time to start thinking about making a change. With the integration of the schools the area had changed radically: it had once been a middle class predominately Jewish neighborhood. However I now was very much a minority, an exotic person. Nine of the thirteen homes in our cul-de-sac had been sold to younger families of various ethnic backgrounds, none white and certainly none Jewish. One morning as I left for work, several of the women were gathered in front of the house next door to mine. They were chatting and laughing in a most friendly manner. Admirably, they had formed a community and I was not part of it. I was the wrong age and the wrong ethnicity. I no longer belonged there.

There really is a time and place for everything and it was time for us, in our late fifties to start to scale down. I was five years into my second marriage, and the children were on their own. Who wants a house, with all of its maintenance? An apartment would do just fine. But that was easier said than done. The times were changing and rentals had become very scarce. Landlords were warehousing apartments in anticipation of converting to co-ops and I was beginning to worry. I had a buyer for my house and would have to get out in two months. Where was I going to go? I had visions of leaving my lovely home and moving into an apartment on a commercial street above a store.

On one of our early trips to Europe, traveling in Copenhagen we were quite surprised to learn that most people either owned or strived to own their apartments. That concept was strange to us. To our knowledge apartments were places that one rented and homes or houses were what one bought. How could you own an apartment? You couldn't chop out a segment of a building and say, "this is mine." In fact, generally speaking in view of the fact that most buildings in our area converted from landlord owned to co-ops, in a co-op, you do not own your apartment. You own shares in a cooperative with a proprietary lease on the space, or apartment that you will occupy. And that's exactly what we did. We bought shares in a co-op and acquired a spectacular apartment.

Miraculously, one Sunday morning in the New York Times, there was an ad for a two bedroom, two bath co-op in a very desirable building in Hewlett at a price we could handle by stretching a bit. We raced over, fell in love, made an offer ten percent below asking price which was accepted and a new era of apartment living was about to begin. The change from homeowner to apartment owner was remarkable. We felt free to come and go and not worry about "the house." That was somebody else's job, no longer ours.

It was really gorgeous – 1200 square feet, which is quite commodious for an apartment. We furnished it with great panache. We had two white leather sofas and a huge white wool rug over which sat an oblong black slate table. It was quite stark and the feeling in the room was softened by a long low rosewood music center, an antique rocking chair accompanied by an 18th century sewing table, a wood and

or running to something better? Was it racism or the desire for community – the need to feel as part of something, not an outsider? This journey of introspection gave me the understanding of the natural desire of most human beings to congregate with like-minded people, almost clannishly and I was emotionally driven to find my niche in an atmosphere of people in a socio-economic circumstance similar to mine. Bayswater was once what I referred to as "a golden ghetto." Its character had changed and it was time to move on to the next "golden ghetto," Hewlett.

We loved living in our apartment. One night, after a local movie, we found ourselves in a Chinese restaurant sitting at a table next to a couple who we knew very casually from Bayswater. As often happens, we engaged in conversation, during which they told us that they had heard via the grapevine that we had bought a beautiful apartment. They were right. However the reason they brought it up was because friends of theirs had just sold their house and were looking for an apartment. This was the height of the nouveau style in our community of buying rather than renting, and apartments were at a premium. Very coincidentally, the apartment next to mine was about to go on the market. It was a mirror image of mine with a third bedroom. They were very anxious to see my apartment so I proudly invited them to accompany us at the end of the meal. They came, they saw, and they loved it. They advised their friends who came the next day. They bought into the co-op and I now had a new neighbor.

Although we were friendly neighbors and the husband, Dennis served on the Board with Stan and me, we really did not socialize too much. We had our circle of friends, they had theirs, and we were basically young enough so that our friends were not leaving this earth on an almost daily basis as they do these years. And then the dynamic changed. Dennis succumbed to cancer and Barb was alone. Having been in that situation myself I was certainly sensitive to her circumstance and would frequently invite her in for a cocktail here and there of an evening. She was very receptive and we were happy to be of comfort to her. After a while she met a nice gentleman and no longer felt the need for the evening cocktail soiree with us. His name was Sam, and although he was fine looking, a good dresser and all of that, he was impotent. So to fill in the gaps, she became involved with another gentleman, on the sly. This new one, Phil, was something else. She had to talk about him, and so Stan and I became her confidants. Cocktail hour resumed.

In a word, this guy was hot! He was divorced a long time. He was a loner. He traveled all over the world, by himself, and from time to time he would call Barb out of the blue, suggest a light dinner and a long stint in bed. She was deliriously receptive to these covert meetings while maintaining her prim relationship with Sam. She loved leading a double life and could not contain herself without sharing the excitement, and so her cocktail evenings with us were hot and heavy.

She was crazy about this guy, and although she must have understood that he was using her she didn't care. She had convinced herself that he was crazy for her body and that he would never leave her. I will say that looking at photos of her when she was a young girl one would have to admit that she was quite lovely and had a stunning figure. However at seventy and thereafter one could not entertain the same comment. Large breasts contained in a restraint may create a falsely attractive image, but when the restraint comes off what happens to the image?

At any rate, Barb was floating in a bubble. She had Sam to escort her wherever she wanted to go and Phil to satisfy the sexual hunger in her from time to time. But as we all know, bubbles do burst.

Some people feel uncomfortable about thinking of older people as being sexual. Certainly our offspring find it offensive and perhaps most people who have lived a secure married life and have now morphed into roommate status with their partners find that sex is history. However that is not necessarily the case and for those of us who find ourselves embarking on a new life as a single and for my neighbor friend Barb it certainly was not. I have no knowledge what her sex life was like as a married woman, but once she got rolling as a single woman, once she shed the widow's weeds her appetite was voracious. Her boyfriend, with whom she cheated on her regular boyfriend was the perfect candidate, no strings, no commitments, good dinners followed by great sex. But something was wrong. He would never sleep over. "I'm crazy for your body, but no I won't sleep over darling," would not sound too convincing to me, but it was not my ear into which he was purring, and it all felt so good to her. What upset the perfect balance was poor Sam. He got sick, really sick, and he died. Barb felt sad, but hardly bereft.

Her campaign to get more attention from Phil went into

full swing. Although her 80th birthday was already behind her, she was incredibly naïve. She could not recognize a brush-off when it happened. She would call Phil almost weekly with some pretext or another, and although she would report to me that they had a good conversation there would be no suggestion of a date. And then one day, a woman answered the phone. The conversation went something like this:

"Hello, who are you?"

"I am Hyacinth, and who are you?"

"This is Phil's friend, Barb, Is he there?"

"Oh, Barb. I know who you are. No he is not here. Do you want to leave a message?"

"Yes, thank you. Ask him to call me." *Hyacinth?* Barb thought to herself. *Could it be his cleaning person? Perhaps. What kind of name is Hyacinth? He probably won't call back. He never does. He likes when I call him.* That was usually how it went, but not this time. He called back and invited her to have dinner with Hyacinth and himself that very night.

She burst into our apartment all excited, I suggested that she calm down and when she did I asked her why she thought Phil had invited her out to dinner with Hyacinth? It suddenly dawned on her that there was something behind this meeting with him and Hyacinth. I urged her to be prepared. He told her to meet him at the restaurant but would see to it that she got home safely. She got dressed in a very sexy dress that paid homage to her 40DD chest and came in for our approval. She arranged for her grandson to drive her to the appointed place and left very excited with promises to return with a full report later. It was a Friday night.

That night is imprinted in my mind permanently. Not as much as Barb's part of it but because that was the last night that my darling husband, Stan spent in our home with me. He was admitted to the hospital the next morning with severe back pains and died of lung cancer ten days later. However this story is about Barb.

When she came back she rang our doorbell and came in. She looked flushed and confused. She needed help sorting out the sequence of events. As she described it, she got to the restaurant early so she would have enough time to order a martini, a rather strong drink for her. She was more inclined to drink a little bourbon with a lot of ginger ale. While nursing the martini, Phil arrived with Hyacinth. Her suspicion about Hyacinth was fairly accurate. The woman was tall, slim, young, and black. The saving grace was that she was not beautiful, not in Barb's eyes anyway.

Phil seated himself between the two women and as Barb related it, all of the conversation was essentially between her and Phil. Hyacinth was silent but observing the two of them. Barb, of course, was thrilled that Phil was paying so much attention to her. She didn't get it. She had no clue as to what was happening and why this little scenario was playing out. She was feeling lightheaded from the unaccustomed Martini and flattered by the attention. I waited to hear the rest of the experience before bursting her bubble.

When dinner was over, Phil brought the car around and Hyacinth jumped into the back seat, ignoring Barb's protestations. When they arrived at Barb's apartment building, Phil got out of the car, opened the car door, said goodnight to her at the car and left. She told us that she was hurt that he did not walk her to the door. She still did not get it, "How could he desire that skinny, flat chested, black, homely woman over me?" she whined. "He met her at the Freeport Community Center. They both like to swim. Big deal. Maybe he figures she'll take care of him if he gets sick. She's a nurse. I'm sure he'll come back to me."

"Barb, don't get your hopes up to high," I cautioned.

"Why do you think this evening happened the way it did?"

"I don't really know. What do you think?" she asked me rather innocently.

"Okay, I'm going to tell you what I think, but first a question. Is Hyacinth living with him?" I said. Her answer surprised me.

"Gee, I don't know. I never thought to ask and they never said anything."

"Well this is what I think. They are living together. She knows how you two were in the past. She does not appreciate your calling him. He assures her that whatever you two had is in the far past. She does not believe him when he says you are just an old woman and were a good lay. He tells her you could not hold a candle next to her. She knows his past reputation as a womanizer and doesn't accept his story and so he calls you right back and invites you to have dinner with them so she can observe the show and recognize that what he said is true. He will never call you again unless he breaks up with Hyacinth."

He didn't.

The tears and heartbreak that started that night continued for months until she met Jack. He was even younger than

Phil. He was fifty-nine. She was eighty-three. He was very hot and she was even hotter.

On Wednesday, Friday and Saturday nights there are weekly dances for elderly people, people who love to dance in spite of their age. For Barb, these became the focus of her life, especially after she met Jack at one of these socials. This man was an opportunist and knew how to take advantage of older, lonely women. He had some kind of menial job in a hospital and was living with an eighty-year-old widow who he had met at a dance. Inasmuch as she did not like to watch him dance around with all of the other women and she did not have the ability to keep up with him, they had an arrangement. He could go to the dances without her but had to come home every night. If he wanted that roof over his head he had to live by her rules, which he did. However, he was clever enough to devise a system whereby he could have his little dalliances and not overtly violate the contract. He would call Barb once a week or so, tell her he would be at her home at 7:30 the next morning but that he had to leave at 3 p.m. Those were the hours he would normally be at work.

As she reported to me, he would dash up the steps, rush

into her arms, and all but carry her into her bed. Well, they would be there for hours. At the very onset he took her out to lunch. Once even a movie, but that was it. Her grandson had a Bar Mitzvah shortly after she met Jack, and when she told her daughter she wanted to invite an escort so she would have a dance partner, her daughter agreed. However, when the family saw Barb acting coquettish, flirting, and cozying up to Jack, they were dismayed. This guy was a few years younger than Barb's son. I must say that I was a guest at the party, privy to the scene and when Jack invited me to dance with him. Barb cut in and let me know that he was hers. I was living with Paul, very happy in my situation and had absolutely no interest in Jack, but by now Barb was obsessed with him and appropriately insecure.

This affair went on for well over a year, although his phone calls and visits became more and more infrequent. She would call his cell phone around the time that she knew he was en route home from work, but he would rarely answer or return her calls. She became more and more devastated. She would see him at the dances, dancing around with all of the women and she would ask him if he would give her a dance. That's how she put it to him; would he give her a dance?

Sometimes he would deign to dance with her and other times he would not. When he did he would lead her on with his before described behavior, whispering sweet nothings in her ear and she would convince herself that he really cared deeply for her and his passion for her was everlasting. He would tell her that he told everyone that there was nobody as terrific as she was in bed. This behavior was like Jr. High School revisited and she, poor fool, took it as a compliment.

Around this time the woman with whom he lived went into a nursing home. He was able to stay in the rent-controlled apartment and the bird was out of the cage. He became involved with one of the regulars at the dance, a woman of obvious means and after a short while they announced their engagement. By now those delicious promising phone calls had stopped totally and Barb was absolutely despondent. She continued going to the dances, hiring a driver for she was no longer driving, and hungrily watching Jack and his intended dance around. Occasionally he would come alone and the routine would ensue. Even though I tried to convince her that this was self-torture, she insisted that it gave her pleasure just to watch him dance and then she would go home and look at the many pictures she had of him and fantasize.

By now, I was no longer living near her and somehow I am not too sure that what I am about to describe really happened. She said that he called her and told her he wanted to come over but that it had to be a secret. She could not tell anyone. She said he came, they had great sex and when she saw him and his fiancée at the next dance she asked him to give her a dance. When he refused she gave him a dirty look and said to him, "You coward!" and walked away. The next day she had second thoughts about what she had said and she tried to call him. By then he had cut himself off from her completely. He had changed his phone number. It was over.

I don't know if she started melting down before the last incident or if that pushed her over the edge but she was never the same. She became delusional and very confused. The dances were over for her, although when I would visit her she would almost childishly tell me that she was hoping to start dancing again soon. Her full time aide would look at me over her head with a sad smile on her face and a caring raise of the shoulders. I keep promising myself that I will make it my business to get to see her one day soon.

From the time that I became aware of the mystery of life and death, death was the gremlin that haunted me, almost like an obsession. It was justified. Realistically, if my mother never reached her thirtieth year for some reason that nobody in my family could describe and my father never reached his forty-fifth, what right did I have to expect longevity? In the years when the concept of genetics was unheard of we did not ask too many questions. It was accepted that ignorance is bliss but for me ignorance translated into fear. Ironically it was not I who was visited by my gremlin death, but it was the men I loved.

When I was fifty-three years old and Que died, I truly thought that my life would always be bereft of happiness and I would spend the rest of my life alone deprived and abandoned again at the hand of death. I did not know that having lost both parents by the time I was ten would be the very engine of strength at this juncture in my life. I had the courage to move on into the most beautiful and gratifying twenty-five year marriage with Stan Becker, my "bashert," the one meant for me, the one who would escort me into the last phase of my life. When he died, I was seventy-nine years old and I mourned him differently. I was not afraid of being alone and I did not cry for me or my loss. I mourned for him. It broke my heart that his life had to end, that he was the one deprived. He was very special and he left a big hole in the hearts of all of us.

A Later Life
Romance

At that stage of the game, I knew that romantic life was no longer meant for me. I had the good fortune to have experienced two great love affairs and that door was now closed, permanently. I knew I would spend whatever life was left for me alone. I knew it. Wrong, very wrong. I had no idea that there was a man, a very interesting artist waiting in the wings. His name was Paul Livert and very serendipitous circumstances brought him to me.

It never entered my mind when I was seventy-nine years old that I would not live the rest of my life alone. I could not imagine that I would possibly have another romance at that late stage. How wrong I was!

It also never occurred to me that I, Esther Bogen would ever answer a personal ad in the newspaper. Wrong again! I did just that, answered a personal ad in Newsday one Sunday night. The wording intrigued me reading as follows, "Retired musician and musical executive, outside artist would like to meet an intelligent, self-confident, emotionally mature *menchette*." It was the word menchette that got me, and so I made the call. As luck would have it, he was not at home and I left my phone number.

The next evening my cousin, who was a Rabbi, came to my apartment to make plans for the forthcoming unveiling of Stan's headstone inasmuch as we were approaching the first anniversary of his death At this most inappropriate time the phone rang and it was the fellow from the ad. I was so flustered that I just blurted out what I was busy with and promised to call him back. I later learned that he didn't think I would, but of course I did. We talked for a while and made a date.

As we were about to hang up, he said, "By the way, I should tell you that I'm fairly short and rather rotund." What a turnoff that was. However, if I was a menchette I wouldn't hold that against him would I? And so we said goodbye.

We were going to meet for a drink at a restaurant called Mateo's. I selected that place because it was a very short walk from my home and I would not have to get into my car, his car, or anyone else's car. Also, it felt safe because there were always a few parking valets around and I felt if anything did not feel right, one of them could walk me home.

Meeting someone from a personal ad was a new experience for me and I did not know what to expect. It was crowded and noisy at the bar so I decided to wait outside. A shabby looking car pulled up and a very tall man got out. Was this the guy or wasn't it? He was easily six-foot-three, and quite good looking, but not attired in sartorial splendor. In other words, he needed a woman's touch.

He walked over to me, a huge smile on his very generous mouth and said to me "You must be Esther. I'm Paul."

My closest friends, Marge and Saul did not like Paul and they made it clear to me. They only saw his surface. He was somewhat scruffy early on and a bit less sophisticated than his predecessor in my life to whom they were sincerely devoted. But that page had turned, he was no longer alive and I was.

Even though we were brought up in approximately the

same period, Paul's life was very different from mine. As a five year old, he had a stint in theater travelling around the country with his uncle who was in a troupe of entertainers. When he was twelve years old he formed a band with himself as the drummer and lead singer. In the 1920s, Fred Trump built attached private homes in Brooklyn, introducing "finished basements." It was a phenomenon and some of the owners rented those basements to groups of boys for very little money to use as a social club. Paul and friends had one such club and it was there that he met his wife to be. He was halfway to thirteen, and she was fourteen. They married when he was barely twenty with his parents' permission.

Although music was his life, and he delighted me with stories of his experience he was also a prolific artist in the Outside Art genre, had a website and was displayed in the Outside Art Museum in Baltimore. What he did using bowling balls as the base was really amazing. What an imagination! His studio was fascinating, loaded with junk from which he created frivolous works of art. His imagination knew no bounds.

Paul was different from anyone I ever knew. I loved that he was so tall. It made me feel protected. He was really big and I could fit under his outstretched arm. As a tall woman, this was fabulous for me, he was wired uniquely, and I loved that. He viewed things through a different prism from mine and as he invited me into his, I invited him into mine.

There was a small café next door to Mateo's and since the bar was not conducive to quiet conversation, we went next door and over a few drinks became acquainted. He told me up front that he lived modestly on a fixed income. To me that translated into dates consisting of a movie and maybe a dinner, which would be a far cry from the theater going I was accustomed to, but then again I did not need him for that. I still had all of our subscriptions to the various Broadway and off Broadway theaters that we supported and to Lincoln Center and so on and went with friends. This fellow was interesting and attractive and an evening here and there could be very nice. In my wildest imagination I could never have foreseen how this would all turn out.

When we first met, he made it clear that money was an issue. To me, marriage was definitely not on my mind so that did not matter. He was a fascinating fellow and I was dating other people, so if he was limited financially it did not matter. I had decided that a movie and a burger with some interesting conversation was a good date. However after a few dates I got a hint that something else was happening. I was in the city at Lincoln Center buying tickets for an upcoming ballet to which I had invited my son and his girlfriend. For reasons I cannot explain the spirit moved me to call Paul and discreetly see if he was interested in going. I told him where I was and what I was doing and that I was not buying the most expensive tickets.

Before I could catch my breath he asked me to buy a ticket for him. This man, an artist, and a musician living on Long Island had never been to Lincoln Center. Neither of us had the slightest idea what was to follow that phone call.

The ballet, *Swan Lake*, was sensational. Although Lincoln Center was one of my regular haunts for as long as I could remember, I have always felt thrilled when sitting in the Metropolitan Opera House, the lights dim and those spectacular chandeliers slowly moving up into the vaulted ceiling. Paul was blown away and that night he realized that for whatever reason, that he had missed out on so much of what is available to us New Yorkers.

Together we stepped onto a magic carpet of exploring the abundance of arts available to us in New York, particularly theater, music, and great restaurants. Paul was a cultural sponge and money became totally irrelevant. The truth of the matter was that he had plenty of it and he had freed himself of the chains of insecurity that had held him back. He moved in with me and once a week went back to his house to make sure that things were in order. When I convinced him that there was no way that I would give up co-op apartment living for the responsibility of a house, he put it up for sale.

He did have some health issues, including complicated heart surgery prior to our meeting, but I didn't care. I knew we would take care of whatever would come when we had to. After nearly three years he was diagnosed with pancreatic cancer which was an enemy against which there was no defense. We were advised not to leave the country and cancelled our cruise to Alaska. Instead, at obscene cost, we flew to Martha's Vineyard and enjoyed a ridiculously expensive spa. Then we went to Santa Fe with my daughter and her husband, a place he had always wanted to see. There too we went to a great spa, enjoyed the hot springs and the massages and I watched his energy and appetite evaporate. I had been advised to expect it and worked hard to keep his spirits up, although we both understood what was happening. By the time we got home he was seriously ill but I did not put him into a hospital to die. I brought hospice into my apartment and kept him as cheerful and comfortable as possible with the help of morphine until he left me.

When he had realized how sick he was and that there was no road back, he put his affairs in order. Instead of putting me in his will he had taken half of his money and put it in his name and mine and the survivor owned the accounts. Likewise, when he sold his house he did the same thing. He arranged it so that nobody could contest what he had done. I had given him a new life and he secured the comfortable continuation of my life after he was gone. I can only look back at the Paul years, short as they were, not quite three, with gratitude for the fun, excitement and extraordinary love that I experienced.

When Paul died I was approaching my eighty-third birthday. I clearly understood that this time was it. I had really left the two by two worlds. In general women outnumber men and in the elderly single society women outnumber men by something like seven or eight to one. Sadly a good proportion of the men are no longer viable. So be it. I would mourn the loss of a great companion and

I would also mourn the loss of a wonderful way of life and find a new path alone. The writing was on the wall, right? Wrong again.

During my years with Paul, I had become friendly with a lovely patient who came to the office regularly. She was a wonderful classical pianist/teacher and we discovered that we both followed the career of an extraordinary accomplished and charming young violinist, Joshua Bell. We found that we were about to attend the same concert, which led to a pre-concert dinner with Paul. This led us into a warm, caring friendship. Shortly after Paul died, she approached me, asked permission to speak on a personal level and told me that she had a gentleman friend who was recently widowed. He was going off to a pre-arranged Florida vacation and she felt very strongly that we should meet before he went. It is common knowledge that the female widowed population in Florida is huge and any unattached man is fair game. Dear sweet woman that she is, she just wanted me to have the edge. She had set up a lunch date for us with herself, her husband and her friend for the day before he was leaving. She cajoled me into accepting the invitation and admitted that she had to cajole the gentleman as well. This was for January 31 and he was leaving February first.

We met at Stresa on Northern Blvd.; a pretty classy place for lunch, particularly for a first date. When Stanley arrived, a few minutes after we did, I really liked the way he had put himself together. I could not know whether it was he or his late wife who had the good taste but it had the scent of Brooks Brothers and it appealed to me. Conversation flowed easily for the next two hours or thereabout and when we prepared to leave the restaurant I mentioned that a film, "The Queen" was showing at the Malverne theater and I wanted to see it. A decision was immediately made that we would all go. After the movie, as we were saying our goodbyes Stanley gave me a very warm, almost intimate kiss on the lips. *Mmm,* that was really nice, I decided. Three weeks later, after a few calls from Florida he came home and called for a date.

We were a good fit but there was really a problem. I was "G.U.," geographically undesirable. He lived on the North Shore, Manhasset, and I live on the South Shore, Hewlett, which is a forty-five minute drive. He suggested that he sleep over in the guest room. That would have been okay except that this Romeo was dating two other women and there was no way that I would be part of a stable. I really liked him and did not want to lose him but I would not compromise myself, even though he kept telling me that I was head and shoulders above the others. I told him that when he got rid of the other two ladies maybe he would not have to sleep in the den. Maybe he could sleep in the big bed, the king size bed in my bedroom.

The rest is history. We will soon celebrate the sixth anniversary of that lunch at Stresa and we recently enjoyed our eighty-ninth birthdays together. Although we do not choose to get married with all of its complications, for all intents and purposes we are as good as married and do share that big bed in our bedroom, hopefully for the rest of our lives, this brave man and I.

Fires and Forever Friendships

Living on a main street it is no longer shocking to hear the screeching of brakes and the wailing of sirens as the fire trucks race down Broadway and hurl themselves onto East Rockaway Road. They race into Hewlett Harbor and East Rockaway, communities of one family houses, and those sounds indicate that a neighbor is in trouble. Frankly I never thought that those sounds would ever relate to me. I lived in a double brick apartment house - in my mind virtually a fortress. Even a building like mine was framed in wood, before it was covered with cement blocks and then covered with bricks. But the roof was very vulnerable, and the interior was even more so.

As a firm believer in maintaining the home in which I live, I decided that it was time to refurbish my guest bathroom. It was time to retire the peach colored tiles, a remnant of the 40s. Who better to do this job than the much advertised Bath Fitters? They were a licensed and insured national organization specializing in exactly what I needed done.

The appointed day dawned, January 2, 2007, a Tuesday, my own day of infamy. A clean cut youngish plumber arrived at 8:30 and worked quietly behind a closed door until 3:30 when he left, closing the bathroom door behind him and promising to return the next day at 8:30. About half an hour later the building's super came to see whether or not he could move an outlet for me. He opened the bathroom door and he looked into the opening in the wall where the medicine cabinet had been removed, leaving the bathroom door open.

Suddenly he shouted, "Oh shit! There's a fire up there. Call the fire department!"

I was talking on the phone to Stanley and ran to see where the fire was, but the only evidence was some black charred bits of insulation drifting down.

The balance of this story is a nightmare. He told me that he had to evacuate the building and that I should make sure that I got my next door neighbor out. This was 4:30 in the afternoon and I knew it was her habit to watch Oprah and to perhaps doze off. With difficulty I was able to get her attention and get her and her friend to vacate. What about me? It was a bitter cold windy night. It never entered my mind that this was anything serious, but as I stood on the lawn hatless, purse-less, and wearing an inappropriately light jacket reality struck. This was much more serious than it appeared. I prayed for the sound of fire engines, but it took ten minutes for the firefighters to get organized. The firehouse is all of four blocks from my home, but the firefighters are all volunteers who have to get to the firehouse from work or whatever and that took time. By the time they got there, having to wait for the chief before starting to control the fire, it was totally out of control, jumping from place to place, ultimately completely destroying six apartments.

Early on, if they had allowed me to show the early arrived firefighters where the fire was, I am sure much less devastation would have ensured. But that's not the protocol and so my apartment and next door apartment and all content were destroyed. I believe that it took seven fire companies and three hours to get the fire under control. It was mesmerizing to watch the firefighters break my windows and throw some of my smaller antique pieces of furniture crashing down. Total destruction. After watching from the steps of the church across from my building in total disbelief, one of my nephews, who lives in the Harbor and who saw this on the News, came to rescue me. My loss was complete; virtually everything I ever owned was taken from me by the fire but the saving grace was that nobody was hurt. Had the super not come in to look into the hole in the wall, had he not opened the bathroom door, had he not left the apartment door open, had the fire remained in the rafters unnoticed behind the closed bathroom door instead of being oxygenated by the open doors, we might have all been asphyxiated in our sleep during the night while the fire smoldered in the rafters and I would not be writing this story.

At 8 o'clock this morning, as I languished in bed, savoring the last few moments before starting my day, my peaceful reverie was disrupted by the gut wrenching wail of the fire house siren. I was immediately alert - virtually holding my breath to see how long it would take for further action. At 8:04 the police sirens sped past my apartment. Tense and waiting - 8:11, 8: 12, 8:13 - yes there they were. I heard the first truck responding and then the second and now the fire chief. A neighbor is likely in a panic, waiting the requisite time for the volunteer firefighters to get from their homes or businesses to the firehouse, to put on their protective gear, to mount their trucks and to rush to their destination.

Childishly I wished that I could be on one of those trucks to get to the scene and help comfort the victims. I would assure them that as long as they escaped unharmed physically, even if they lost everything, they would survive and be grateful. I would not tell them about the traumatic aftermath. No, I would not tell them what it was like after waiting five days to finally be allowed to enter my apartment, my beautifully furnished home, and see the wreckage with my own eyes; the wet dank smelling rubble that was once my peaceful sanctuary. My precious off-white Aubusson rug was black and sopping wet covered with debris, my beautiful antique rocker, chopped up and unrecognizable, my rosewood Victorian sewing table destroyed, my collected artwork hanging askew or thrown on the floor stomped on or slashed, my hundred year old Spanish dining table hacked and water logged, my stately king size bed playing host to broken night stands, my kitchen utilities torn away from their moorings and thrown on their sides, drawers pulled out and contents strewn all over, the den impassable. No I would not tell them about the total destruction of my lovely home, now looking as if a bomb had exploded in its midst, clothing and everything personal gone, enveloped not by fire but by water used to put out a fire raging in the attic space above the apartments.

I would not tell them what it was like to suddenly understand what it feels like when you realize that you are homeless. Homeless. "If you have no place to go, we will put you up in a hotel," the kindly Red Cross people offer. "It's cold out, you can sit in the church," the kindly priest suggests. "If you need to make a phone call, you can use my cell," a kindly onlooker offers. No, I would not tell them this part. I would not tell them how difficult it is to reconstruct a life starting from zero. I would only tell them what everyone told me, much to my chagrin, "They are only things and can be replaced. I know. I've been there and done that."

Serendipity. A niece learned from a friend that her aunt had died and her apartment was for sale, just across the street from my former home. It certainly was not my plan to own two apartments, but under pressure from my children I caved, and much to my current delight bought the apartment in a building with all kinds of amenities in which I now live in comfort. Although my former apartment, which had been restored beautifully, is idling waiting for the right person with courage to buy in this market, to come along and fall in love with it, I remain optimistic and marvel at the resiliency of the human mind. It knows when to dull and it knows when to shine and here I am telling you about it, superficially of course, and my voice isn't even quivering.

———————

Sometimes I am amazed at what triggers a particular memory. It could be anything as fleeting as a scent or a voice. This happened to me recently, in a supermarket. A female voice made a comment about the price of corn, "They should be ten for a dollar at this time of year, instead of forty-nine cents each."

I could have sworn it was my friend Jane speaking, although I knew she had been dead for a few years. As I turned to see whose voice it was, the woman walked away and I never saw her face. But the voice had done its job. It took me back sixty years.

Wendy was a few weeks old. It had been a great triumph to maintain the pregnancy after two miscarriages and to bring it to fruition. After that, a life threatening hemorrhage was skillfully overcome and I was in a very happy place. My doorbell rang and I opened to find a lovely looking stranger with a small boy in tow.

She was about my height with red, short, curly hair, and the brightest blue eyes, "I know you don't know me," she said, "I live around the corner next to your sister-in-law. When I heard that you had your baby and are now well, I had to come and congratulate you and tell you how happy I am for you." Of course I invited her in. that was the beginning of a close friendship that lasted well over fifty years.

Jane was an only child, the product of a tempestuous marriage torn apart by an ugly divorce. Her childhood was spent with her mother whose second and third marriages also ended in divorce, and whose fourth marriage was waiting in the future. Her father, a gentleman of means, lived in the area, but Jane was not permitted any contact with him. If she called him and was caught, her mother would stop speaking to her for days on end. She was a lonely child and yearned for a big sister. That yearning carried into adulthood and there I was, a few years older than she.

Jane's mother, Lilly, owned a hat shop in the area. She was a very flashy woman who always walked around town with a hat on, regardless of heat or humidity. She wore her hats well and advertised them at no cost. She was a sharp entrepreneur both in her business enterprise and her selection of husbands. She knew how to buy and sell. She also knew how and when to dispose of unwanted products. Her business prowess and selection of husbands made her a rich woman. Jane was the typical poor little rich girl.

She married Frank when she was nineteen years old. He was a good looking, Air Force Captain, recently returned from overseas. She thought that she was rescued from her mother's domineering clutches and it appeared so for a while. However, a controlling mother with a lot of money is difficult to subdue. A returning serviceman without a specific career can be easily seduced when he has a wife and two children. He was selling diaper service, which was a dying industry. An offer of owning your own business in the town you live in can be very convincing. And so the wheels were turning and fate was watching.

They lived in a modest two-bedroom apartment with two small boys. Frank's job was tentative, at best. The scenario was ripe for Lilly to take over. She offered, in the name of love for her daughter, to establish a "small appliance" store for Frank to run. She also purchased a house and offered it to them for a pittance of maintenance cost. There was no way her generous trap could be refused.

At the beginning it appeared to be working. The store was right in town, diagonally across the street from Lilly's store. It was housed in a building that Lilly had inherited from divorce number two. Lilly was wise enough to keep her distance early on. She let Frank dig his feet in and feel that the store was really his. Both he and Jane did possess good business acumen and she could relieve him for lunch or to go on a buying trip. As far as we, her close friends, could see, things were fine and Jane was lucky that this whole thing had come to her so easily. We were all struggling to establish ourselves and stay afloat. None of us had a rich mother who helped us so generously. We did not see the attached strings that Madam Lilly had started to pull. In her effort to control Frank, who was not having any part of that, she put Jane back where she was as a little girl, between two adults in a no-win fight.

We became aware of the dark clouds hovering over our friends at a New Year's Eve party at their home. They had a large, clubby kind of basement with a fireplace. When we arrived we noticed a carton of champagne glasses near the fireplace. On the bar was a large bucket of ice with several bottles of champagne in it being chilled. This was a bit unusual. We were more accustomed to cheap red wine and spaghetti with meatballs, or rye, rum, and scotch. But this was New Year's Eve and Frank was, after all, in his own business, and could splurge.

What we did not know was that this was their last big blast in that house. When we started drinking champagne, we were told to smash the glasses in the fireplace. We were helping them celebrate the fact that he had told Lilly to take the store and shove it along with the house. Whether or not Jane would have a relationship with her mother was entirely up to her. Frank would not allow that woman to emasculate him and he would take care of his family, no matter what it took.

Around that time, we began to learn of Frank's experience during the war. Our husbands were all retired servicemen.

In our ethnicity, military aspirations were rare, so all of our guys, with the exception of Frank, were draftees. They were in various branches of the army, including infantry, armored engineers, communication specialists, medics, cooks, and paratroopers. All of them had seen combat overseas and all of them had a secret. They just kept it to themselves. They did not want to talk about their experiences.

Frank's story was a little different. When it became obvious to him that his number would soon be called up, he enlisted. He wanted to be in the Air Force and he wanted to be an officer. He could go to Officer Candidate School for ninety days and become a second lieutenant. Those officers were referred to as the "90 Day Wonders." But first, he had to get through Basic Training, and the drill sergeants were as tough on those kids as on anyone else. Perhaps they were even tougher, if that was possible. "Don't think you college fucks are better than anyone else!" they would shout out, "Either shape up or ship out!" But they were different. They were headed for the Army Air Force, the elite branch of the service. They were the "Fly Boys." They wore the coveted fancy leather jacket. And so, Frank became a First Lieutenant, a Bombardier.

The war was raging. Naturally, Frank was shipped overseas. His missions were in Italy. They were carried out at night and they were gruelingly dangerous. The schedule called for twenty-five night missions and then a few days off, to rest and relax. At that point, Frank had completed a twenty-five night tour and was scheduled for resting. When one of his fellowmen crewmen fell ill and the call went out for a replacement, Frank volunteered. He understood that the mission would have to be scrapped if nobody offered to go. These bomber planes served no purpose without a bombardier. They needed him and he agreed to go. As it turned out, this twenty-sixth mission was to be his last. His plane was shot down over a small town in Italy. Frank was discovered by a group of Italian Partisans, elderly men and some women who rescued him, harbored him and nursed him back to health. For the next nine months he was hidden by day and joined them in their acts of resistance by night, until he was reunited with the American forces.

This story, of course, is only a skeleton of Frank's experience, but it was as much as he was willing to divulge. It was really much more than the others would talk about for years. However, Frank would drop bits and pieces of his story when he was drunk.

We all drank, and sometimes too much, but Frank actually got drunk most of the time. He was very funny when he overindulged, and we all laughed with him. One night, he was hosting a small party. He ran out of ginger ale or some such thing, so he and the other two men went to go get some more. Jane wanted to rearrange her living room furniture, but Frank was uncooperative. Taking advantage of his absence, we agreed to assist her. The couch stood to the left of the entrance to the living room. We moved it to a different wall and when the men returned, Frank was so impervious to his surroundings; he sat right down where the couch used to be, right on the floor. He was inebriated enough not to feel anything and to hardly realize what had happened. None of us, including Jane, realized that Frank had a serious problem. We did not anticipate that it would exacerbate over time and take over his life.

After that big New Year's Eve party and the throwing of the champagne glasses at the fireplace, Jane and Frank moved out of the big house that Lilly owned. They moved into a small apartment, and Frank locked the door to the store and gave Lilly the keys. He took a job as a floor boy in a department store. It was a fortuitous move. A Manhattan store, South Klein's at Union Square decided to open a store in Hempstead. Frank took a low end job in their small appliance department and within three months he was the manager of the department. He then became the buyer. Within a few years, they opened another store in Farmingdale. They offered to move him up, but he elected to stay where he was. He knew there would be bigger fish to fry and when they opened a store in Silver Springs, Maryland, they offered him the top job of Store Director. That position was worth the move. At that time, fifteen thousand dollars a year was very nice. Frank was making sixty. He had really made it. Life was good, money was plentiful and so was booze! They had a third son, bought a lovely home, and invested in the stock market.

We kept in touch sporadically through the years even though they lived in Silver Springs. Then, things changed. Klein's now had four stores in the New York area and they had over-extended. The Board of Directors brought Frank back to New York to be in charge of the whole New York area. This was a prestigious position with a high salary and a very big headache. At this point, Frank was drinking two or more

Martinis with lunch to help him get through the afternoon when he could go home and do some more drinking.

It took him a long time until he finally admitted to himself that he had a serious drinking problem, but couldn't stop. He started having blackouts and when it happened at work, he decided to consult a psychiatrist. After a period of time the doctor told him that his self-destructive nature combined with the enormous stress he was under from his job and his alcoholism was literally going to kill him. If he wanted to live, he had to get off the merry-go-round, and soon!

Jane's mother, Lilly had moved to Florida. Although there had been a rift, in that family dynamic, such things were not uncommon. The issues were never resolved; they were just ignored or put under wraps temporarily. Ignoring the rift, Jane called her mother, told her of Frank's plight and asked her to find a house for them. Lilly saw this as an opportunity to return to some position of control and did as she was asked. Frank left Klein's, packed up his family and moved to Florida, not knowing what he was going to do next. What he did know was that he was not going to give up drinking, although he promised Jane that he would. In his wildest dreams, he never could have anticipated where his love affair with Vodka would take him.

Years passed. To me, a visit to Florida meant a week or ten days with Jane and Frank at their home. To them, a visit to New York was a week or ten days at my home. This could come about almost every year with an occasional hiatus.

Much changed in my life, but for them things stayed the same. Frank had stopped drinking but was very involved with prescription drugs, the ones that put him to sleep and the ones that helped him stay afloat. He was under the care of two doctors, neither aware that the other existed. With this cunning scheme he was able to get double supplies of drugs, which he ingested regularly. In retrospect, I believe the psychiatrist at the V.A. knew, but he himself was a drug addict who one morning opened the window of his office at the V.A. hospital, and jumped to his death.

Fast forward a few years. My life had changed and I was now in a new relationship with Stanley Rosenfeld. One evening my next door neighbor came into my apartment to join us for cocktails. Both she and Stanley were brought up in Bayswater and they were discussing various people they knew as youngsters. The television news played quietly in the background and I was watching aimlessly when a name popped up in their conversation. To me, it sounded like Rosela.

"Did you say Rosela?" I asked.

"No, Rosela's, but why do you ask?" said Stanley.

"Oh, my friend Jane Strassberg's mother owned a shop in town called Rosela's."

"Did you say Strassberg? My best friend in elementary school was Frank Strassberg. Any connection?"

"Stanley, the sleeper couch on which you are sitting on is the very bed on which Jane and Frank Strassberg sleep when they come to New York. This is really amazing. I am going to call him right now!"

Frank was astonished when I explained to him that Stanley Rosenfeld was there with me. We had a very excited telephone reunion, with Frank and Stanley repeatedly remarking about the amazing coincidence which brought the two of them together after a lifetime of living in separate directions. Jane got on her extension phone and we all agreed that the next day the Strassbergs would look into flights and come to New York in the next few weeks. It was late spring, the weather in Florida was getting very hot and humid, so the timing was great and it would be so wonderful to see each other. We all laughed together and bid each other goodnight. That was the last time I heard Frank Strassberg's voice.

Jane called me the next day and instead of telling me when they would be coming, she told me that during the night Frank got up, as he usually did, took some more sleeping pills, as he usually did, but did not wake up the next morning. He succumbed to an overdose of prescription drugs. Given the amount of abuse his body sustained, first from alcohol and then from drugs, it was quite remarkable that he lasted until just past his eightieth birthday. But Stanley and I mourned the reunion that never happened.

An Impossible Ending

From time to time, because of writing these memoirs, I have visited different periods in my life. By now it is quite evident that the path I travelled had its travails and its rewards. Perhaps some choices could have been better, who knows? What I do know is that I do not entertain any serious regrets but for one: it has to do with my grandmother, my Bubby.

In telling about my life as an army wife, I have previously indicated that when I got to Junction City, Kansas, at Bubby's behest, I located the Jewish USO. Innumerable times I have replayed in my mind the conversation that brought me there. It was Thursday night, the night before I left. We were in the kitchen in the back of the store. Bubby never shed a tear, but her face revealed all of the fears she felt for me. She did not touch me. She told me to sit down and she sat down near me, and this is what she said:

"Ven you'll come in Junction City, Kenses, on der main street dere, on der corner, is a grosser USO. You should not go dere. In der middle from der block, is dere a jewelry store. On top from dat jewelry store is dere a Jewish USO. You should dere. All right?"

Of course, that's exactly what happened. What I had no understanding of then was that her fears for me were based on her reality about anti-Semitism. She knew what was out there, even here in America. I was young and clueless. I would learn later on.

My regret is that I never asked her how she knew to send me there. Today you can turn on your computer, go to Google, and find out anything you want to know; but in 1943? A non-English speaking immigrant somehow or other managed to ferret out information about something she know nothing within the space of a few days and I never thought to ask her how she did it. It remains a mystery and that is my one true regret in life.

cane chair upholstered in black and an antique wooden scrolled side table with lamp. Of course there were several other lamps. I never liked ceiling lights in a living room or bright lights of any kind. I like a living room to have a sexy feeling, and this room did. It had a large arch at one end creating an L shape and that other section was the bar; a small black velvet couch and a sleek black, white and glass breakfront which opened into a bar. This apartment was made for partying and we did. One of my friends coined the phrase that this apartment was "drop dead gorgeous." It was so gorgeous that when you walked in you gasped and nearly "dropped dead." It really had the feel of a sophisticated New York apartment.

It's pretty complicated to buy into a co-op, usually taking about three months. During that period of time I did have some reservations about leaving my house, which I loved, and did some introspection as to why I was doing it. The house was paid for, beautiful, large, comfortable, and full of all kinds of memories. Why was I putting myself back into a mortgage and a much higher maintenance? What had pushed me? Would I ever be satisfied? I really did not like change so the question was, am I running from something

About the Author

Esther Bogen, born in Brooklyn, New York, has spent the past sixty-five years on the South Shore of Long Island.

Her memoirs take us on a ninety-year journey as an orphan during the great depression, an army wife during World War II, deaths, marriages, and even swinging mid-life singlehood. Her life and work are vibrant, touching, insightful, humorous, and always interesting.

After graduating high school at sixteen, Ms. Bogen began what has become her lifelong quest for intellectual growth. Her self-education and introspection continues to this day as she participates in a writers' workshop and three current events discussion groups each week.

This new author's sense of humor and mind are sharp and most can appeal to people of all ages.